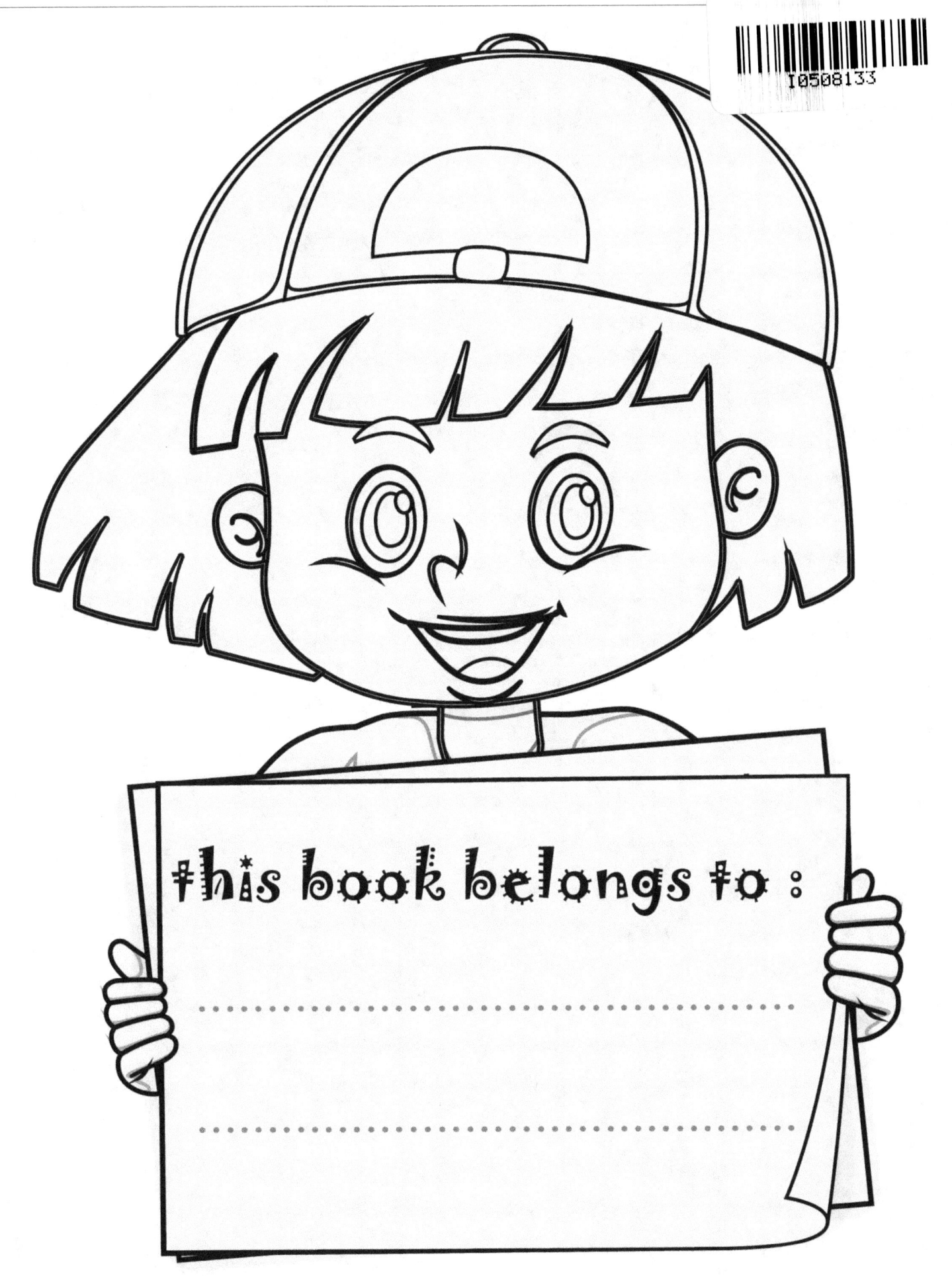

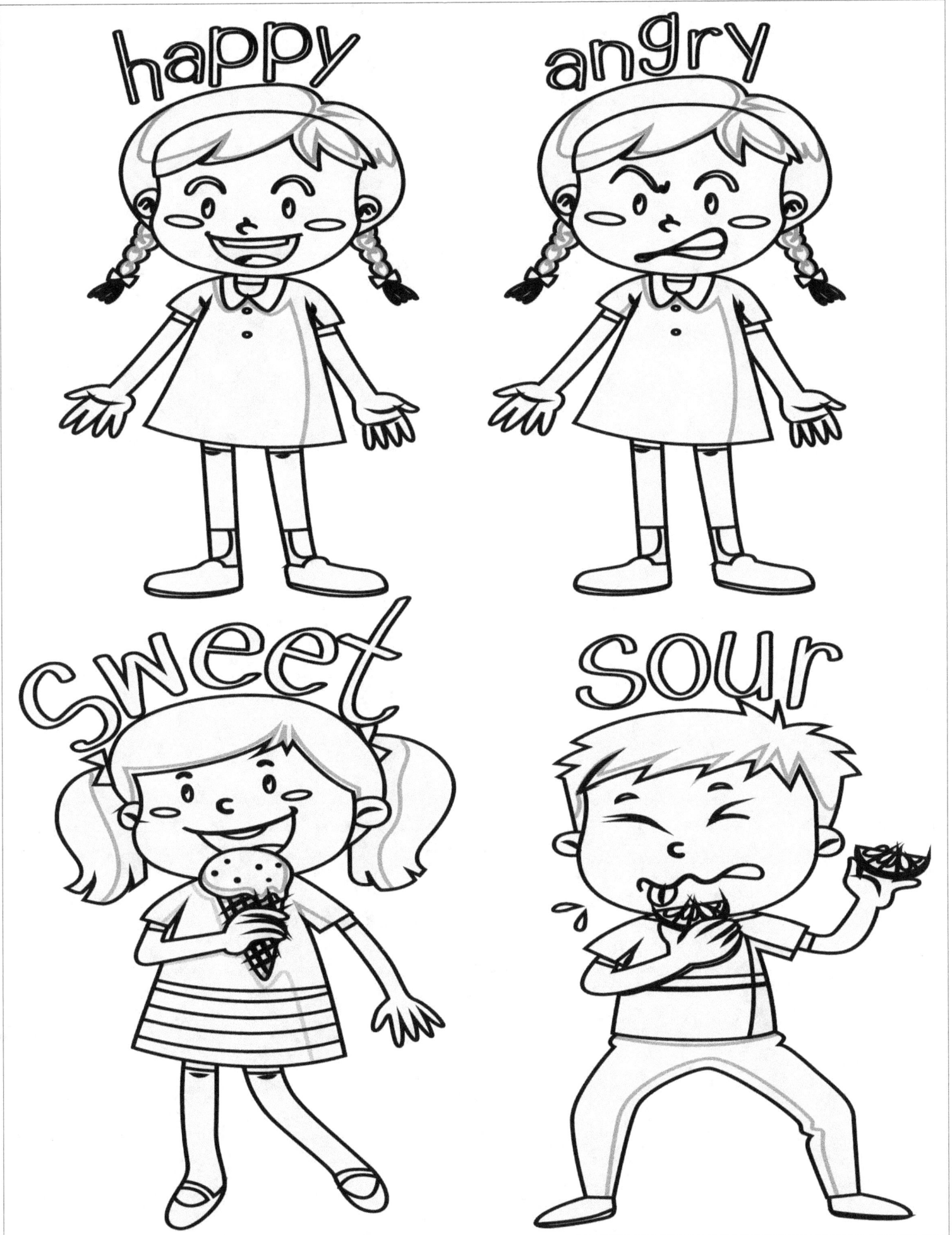

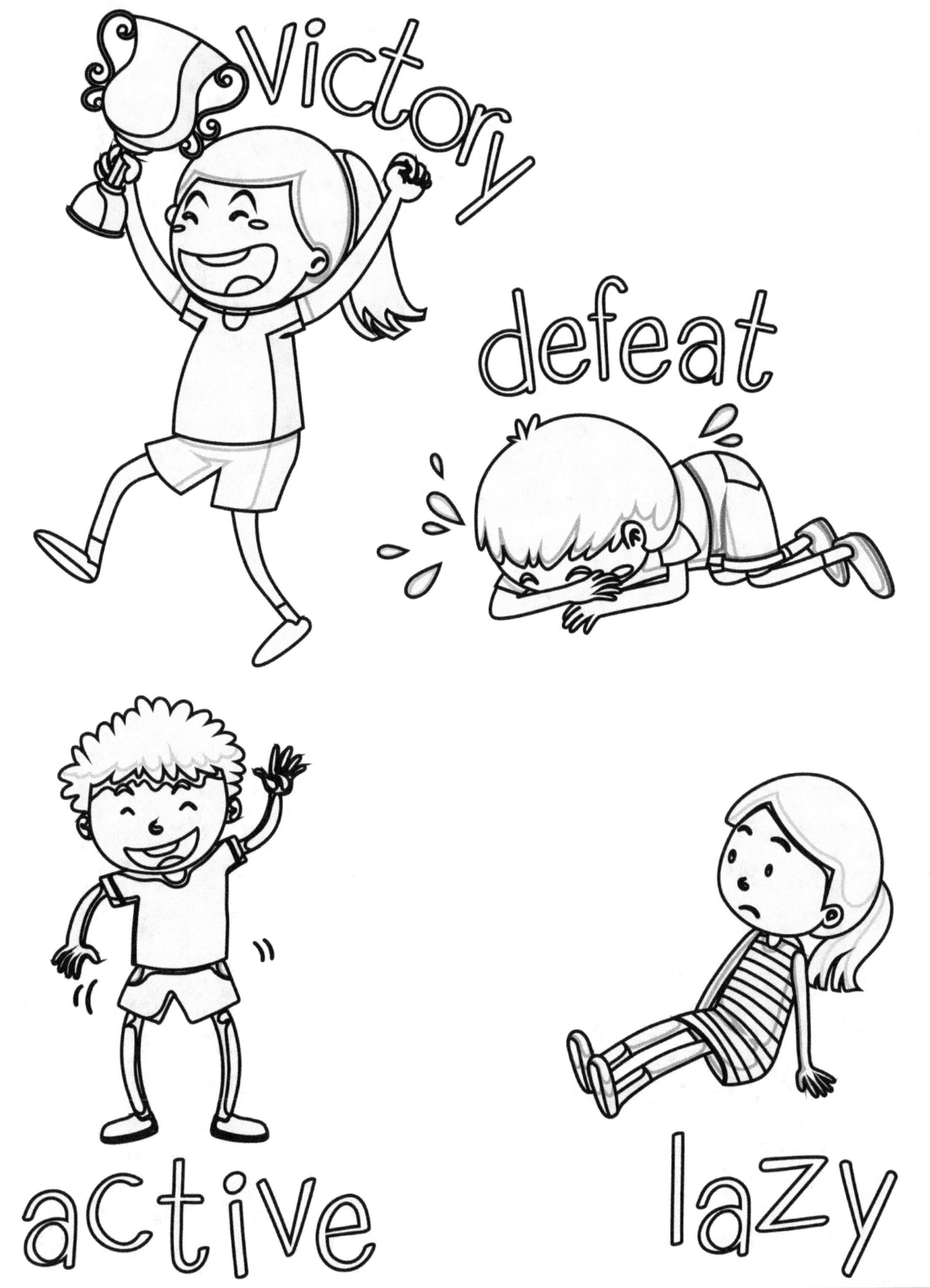

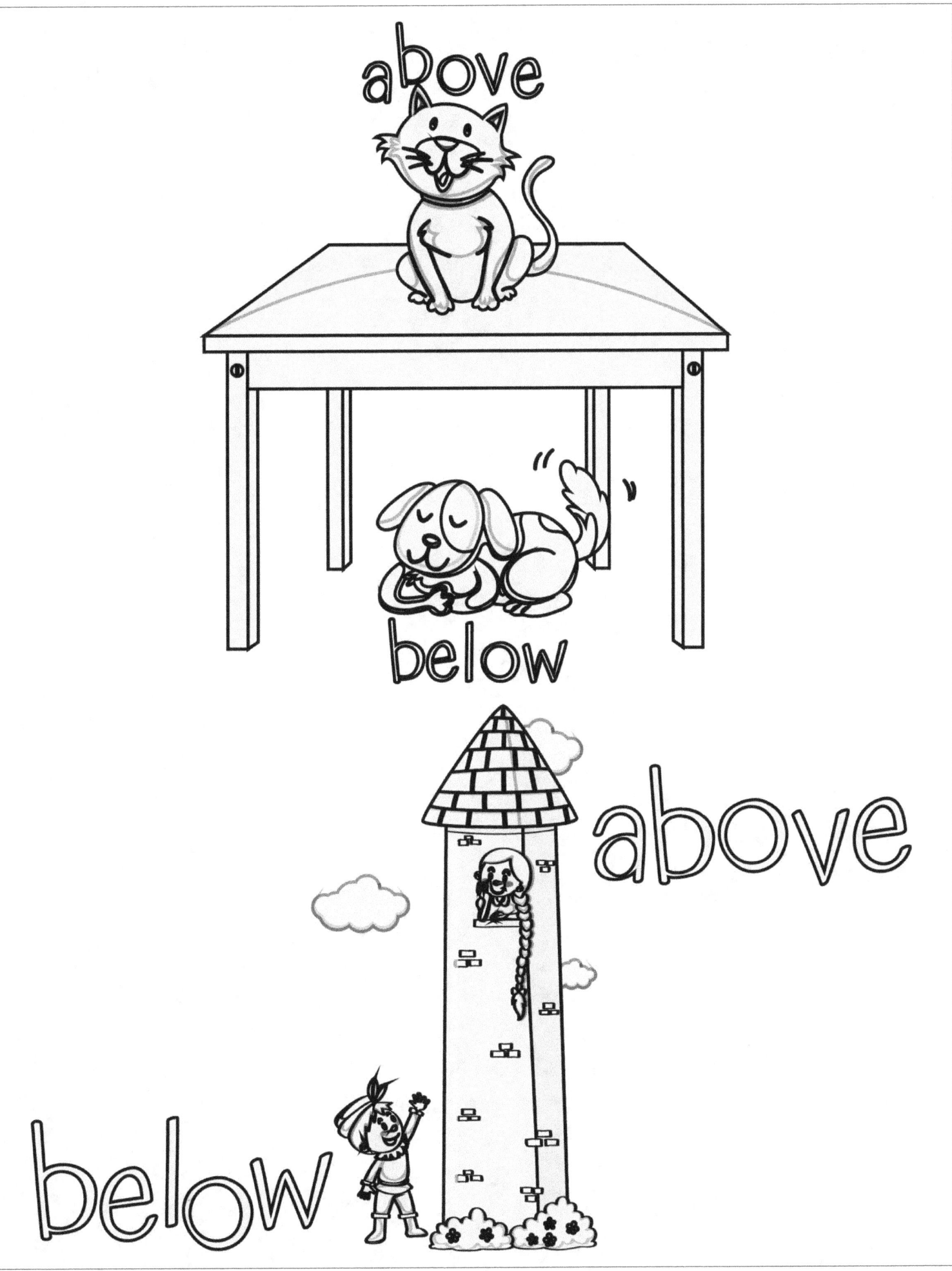

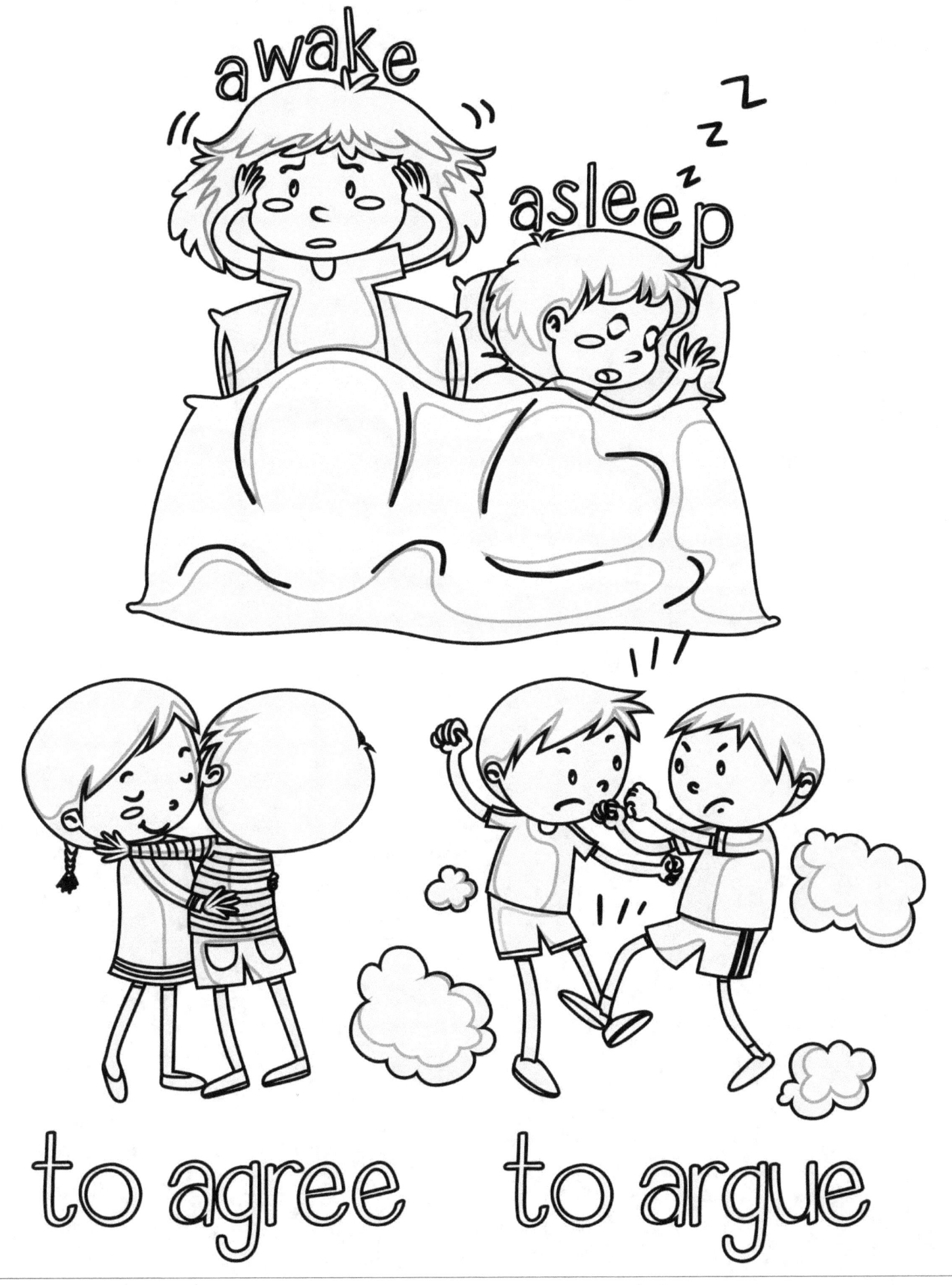

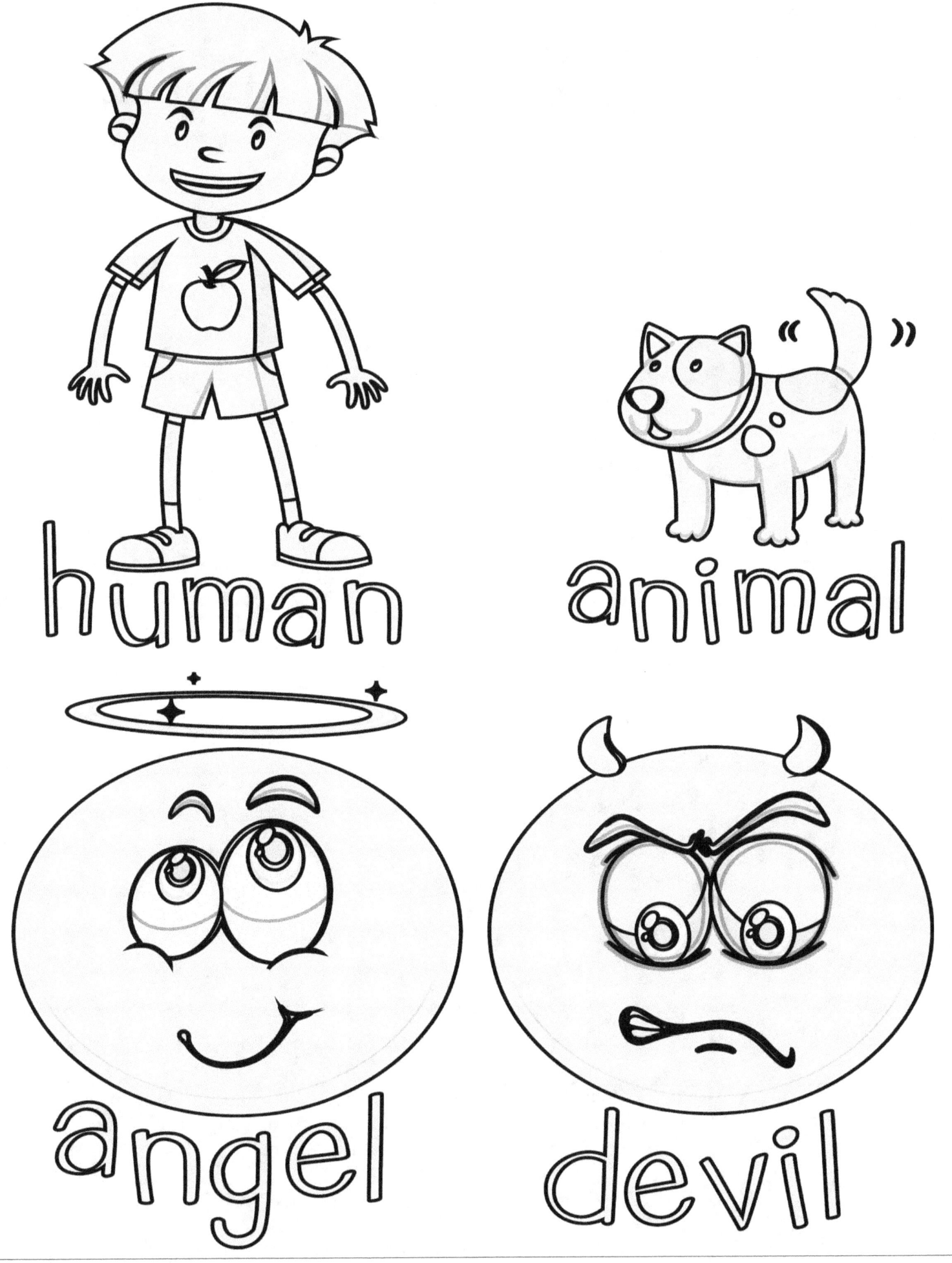

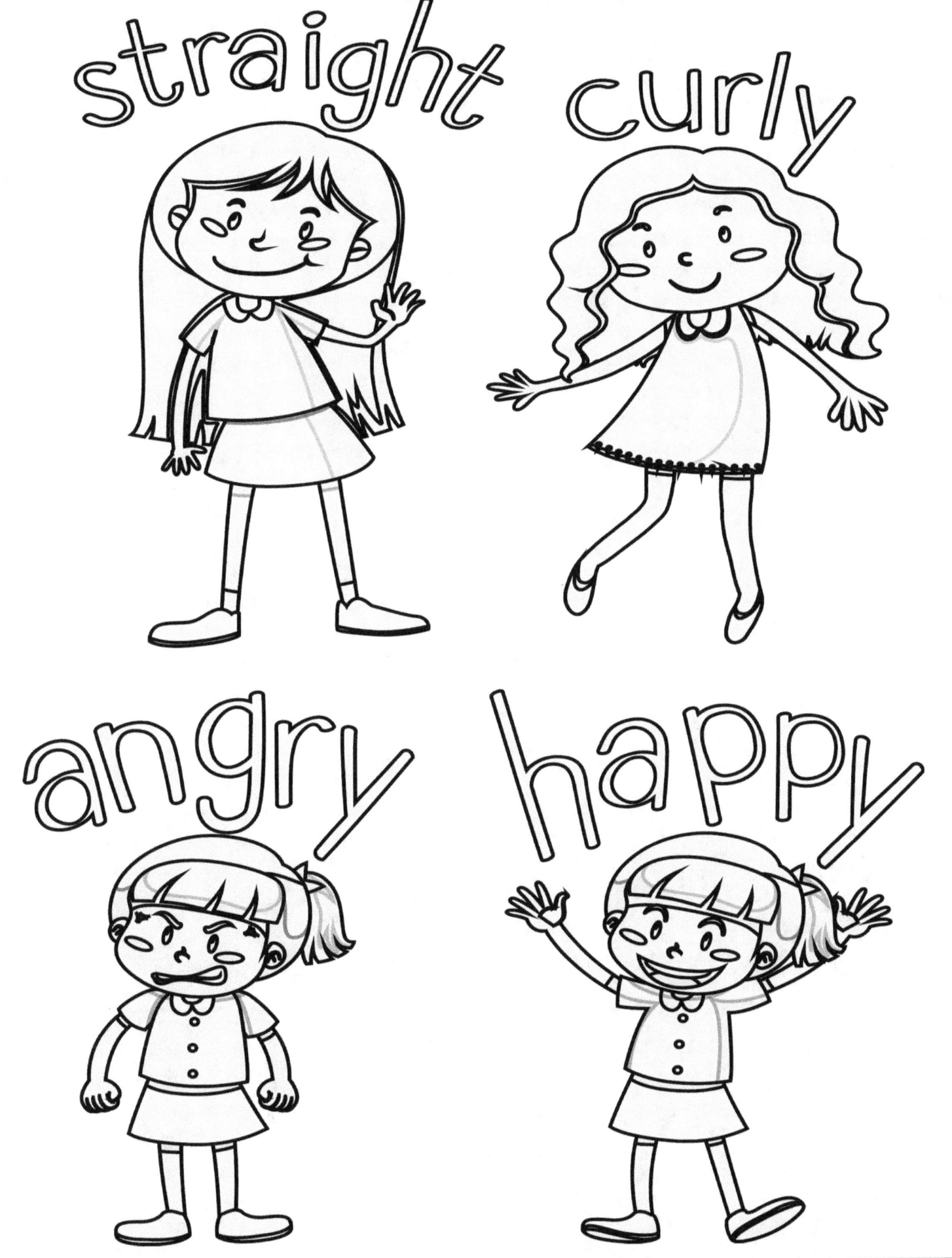

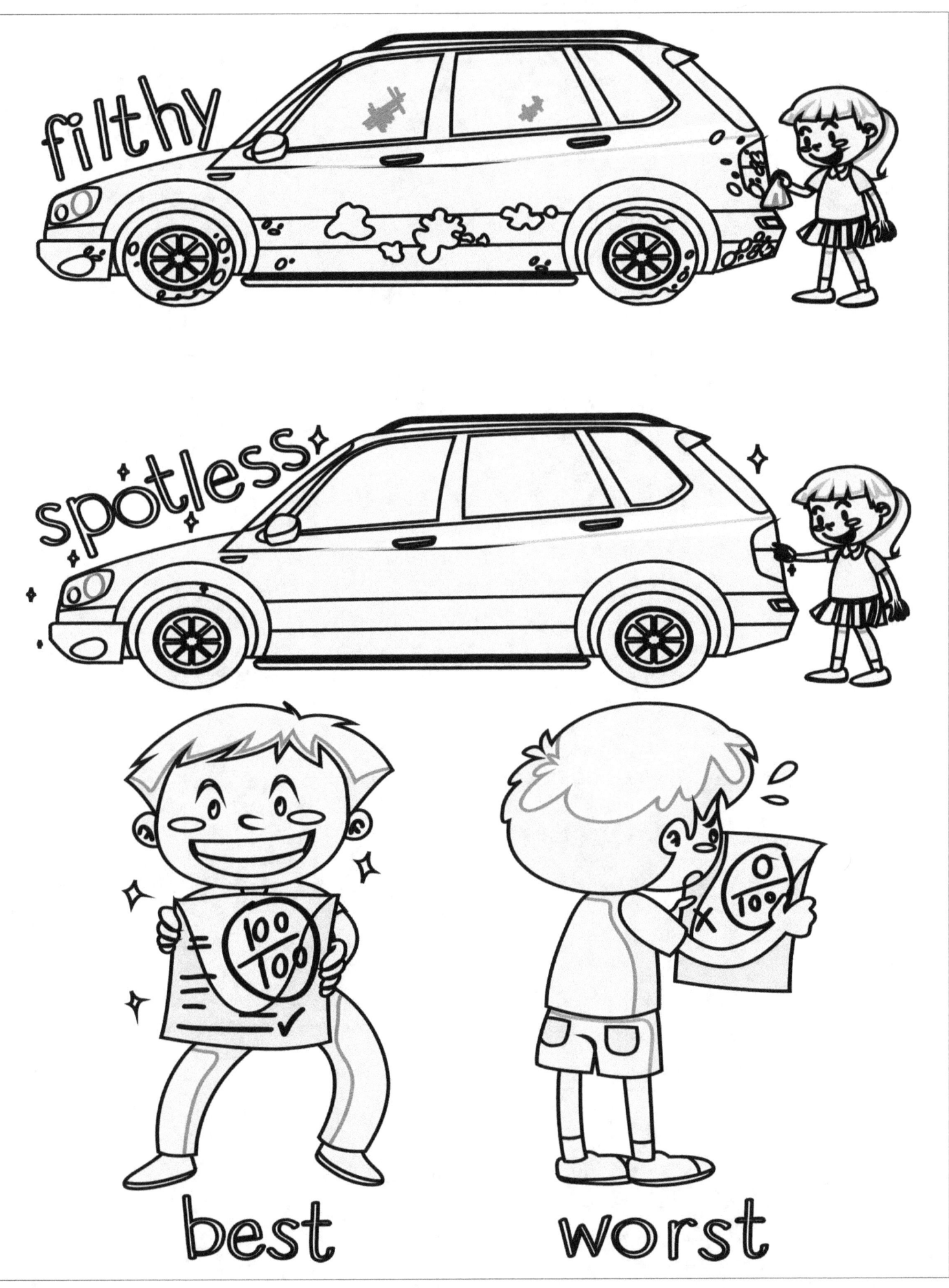

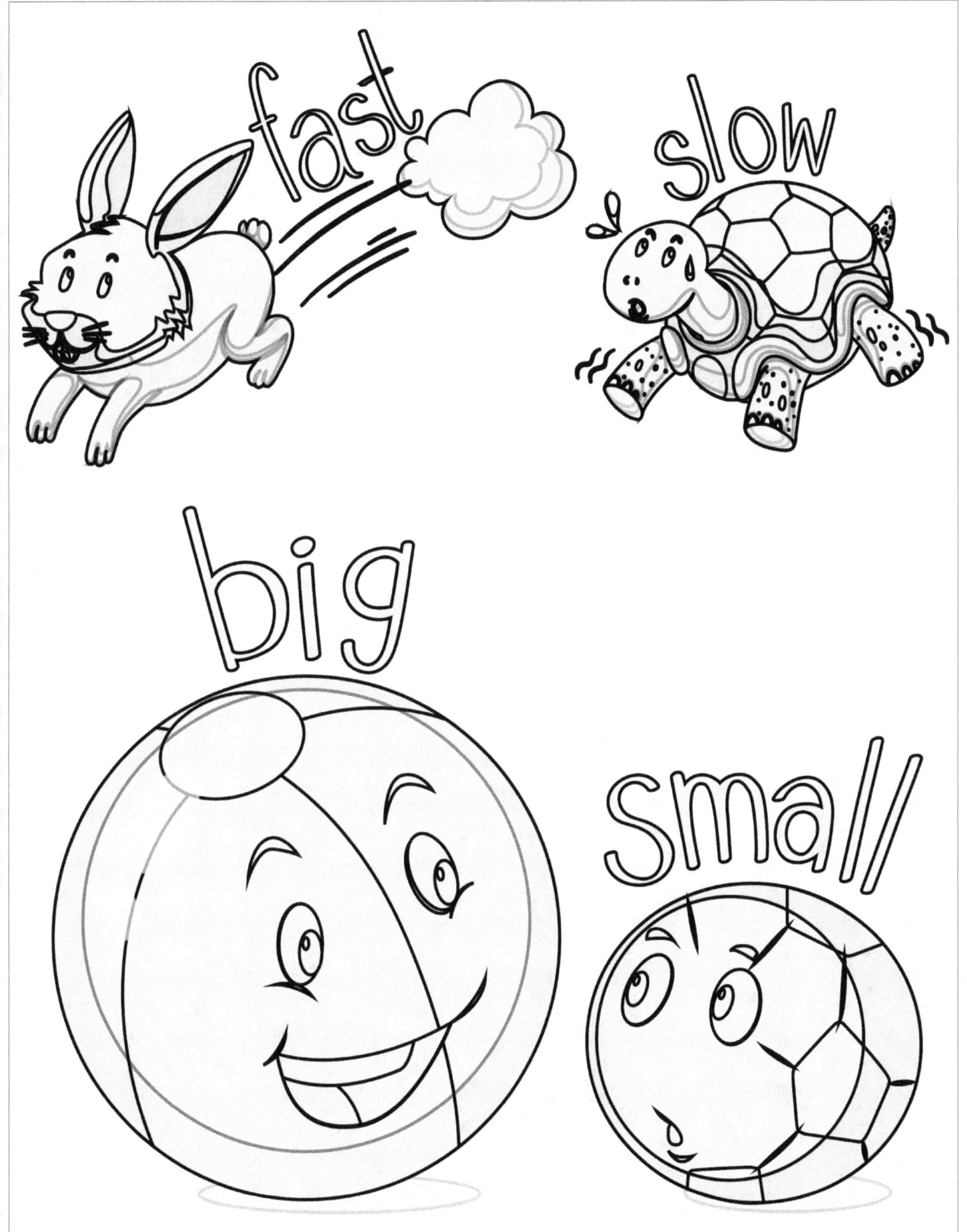

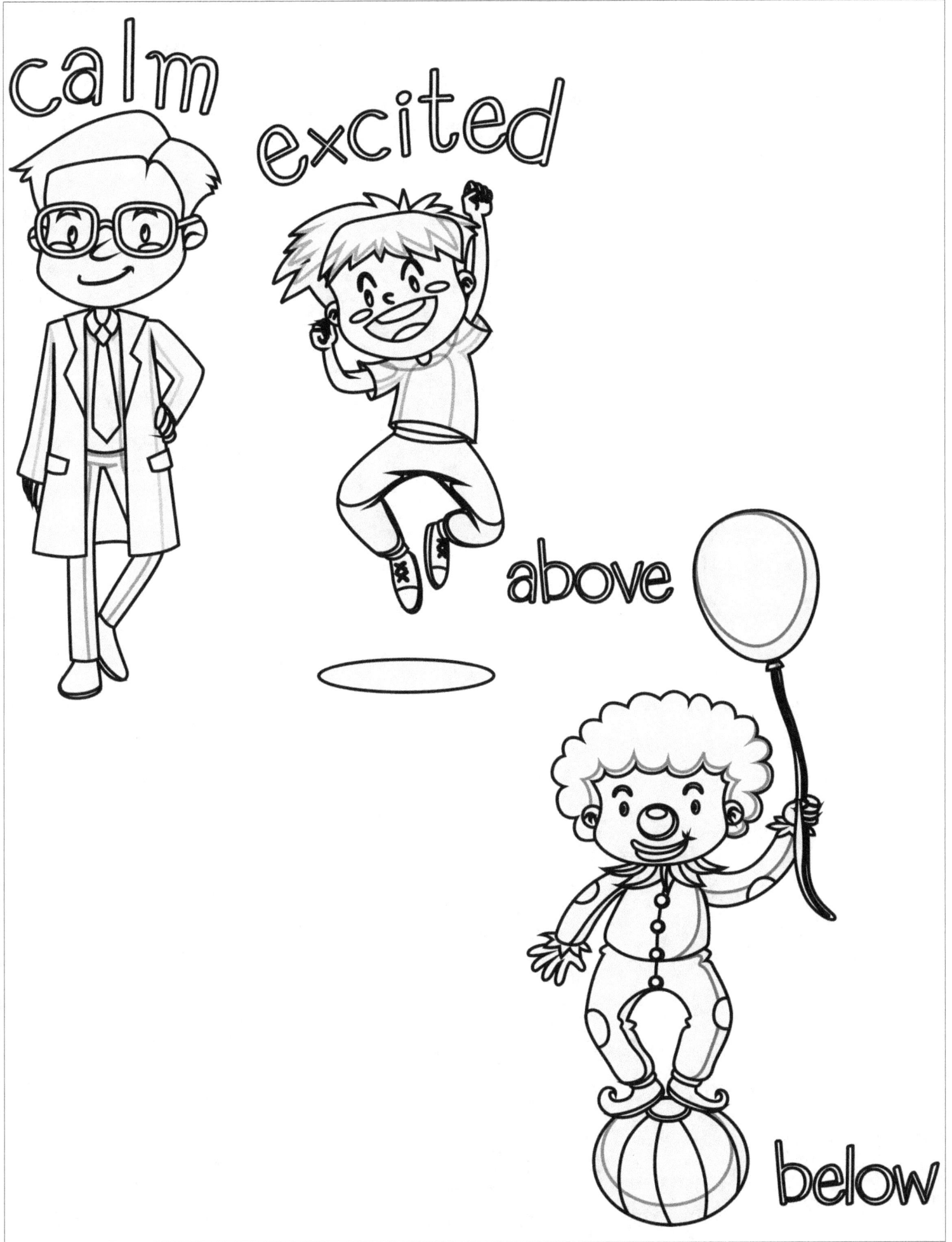

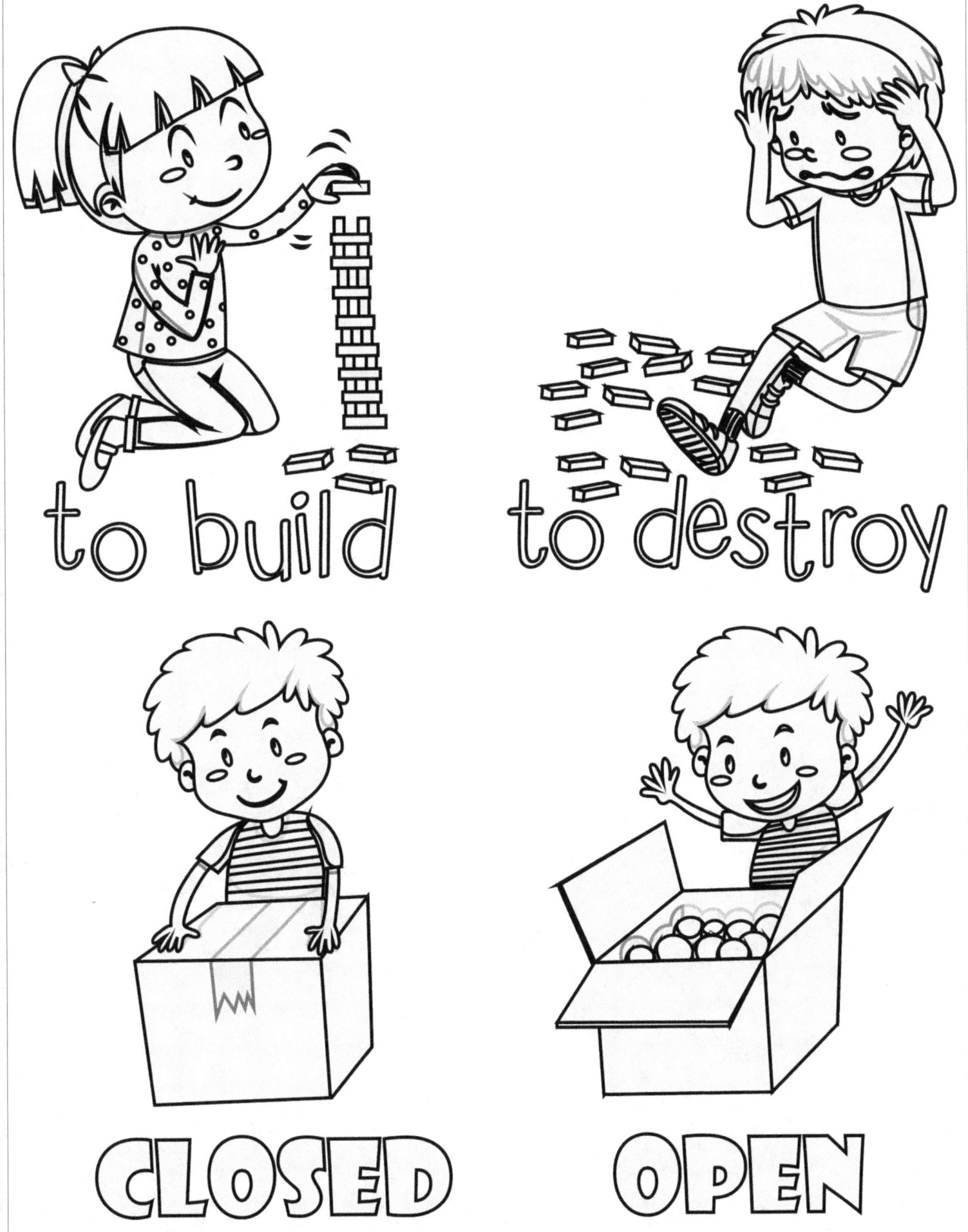

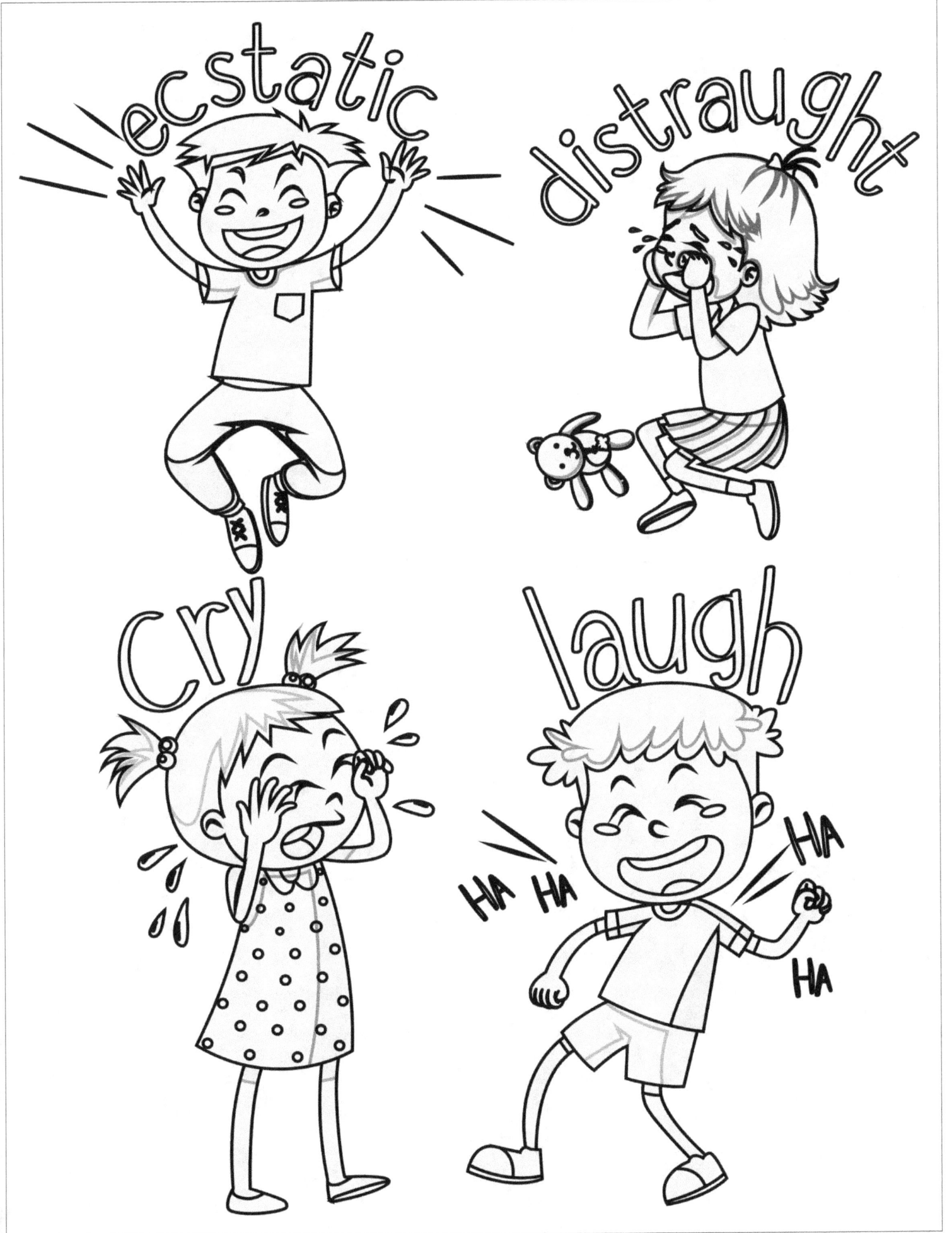

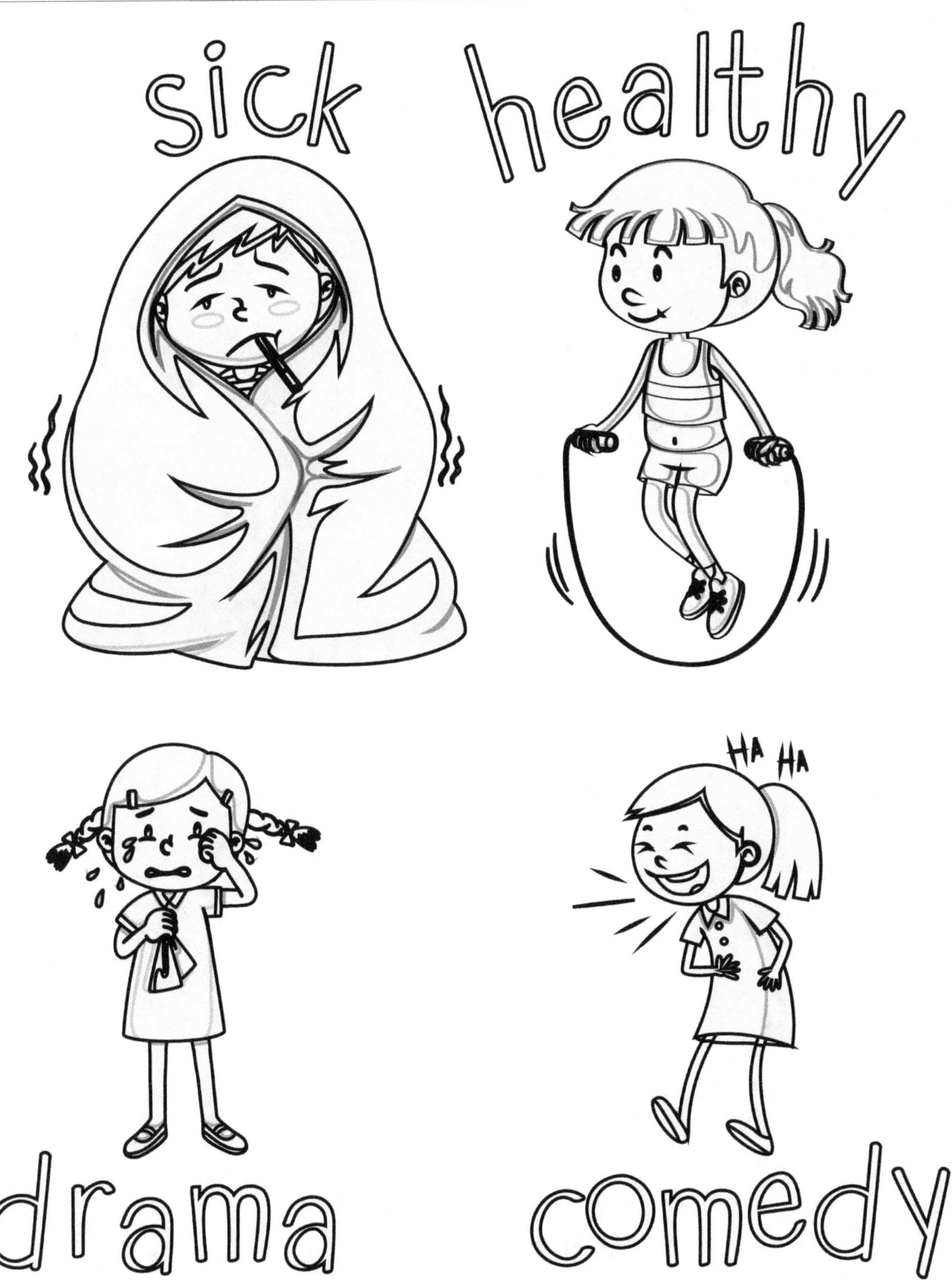

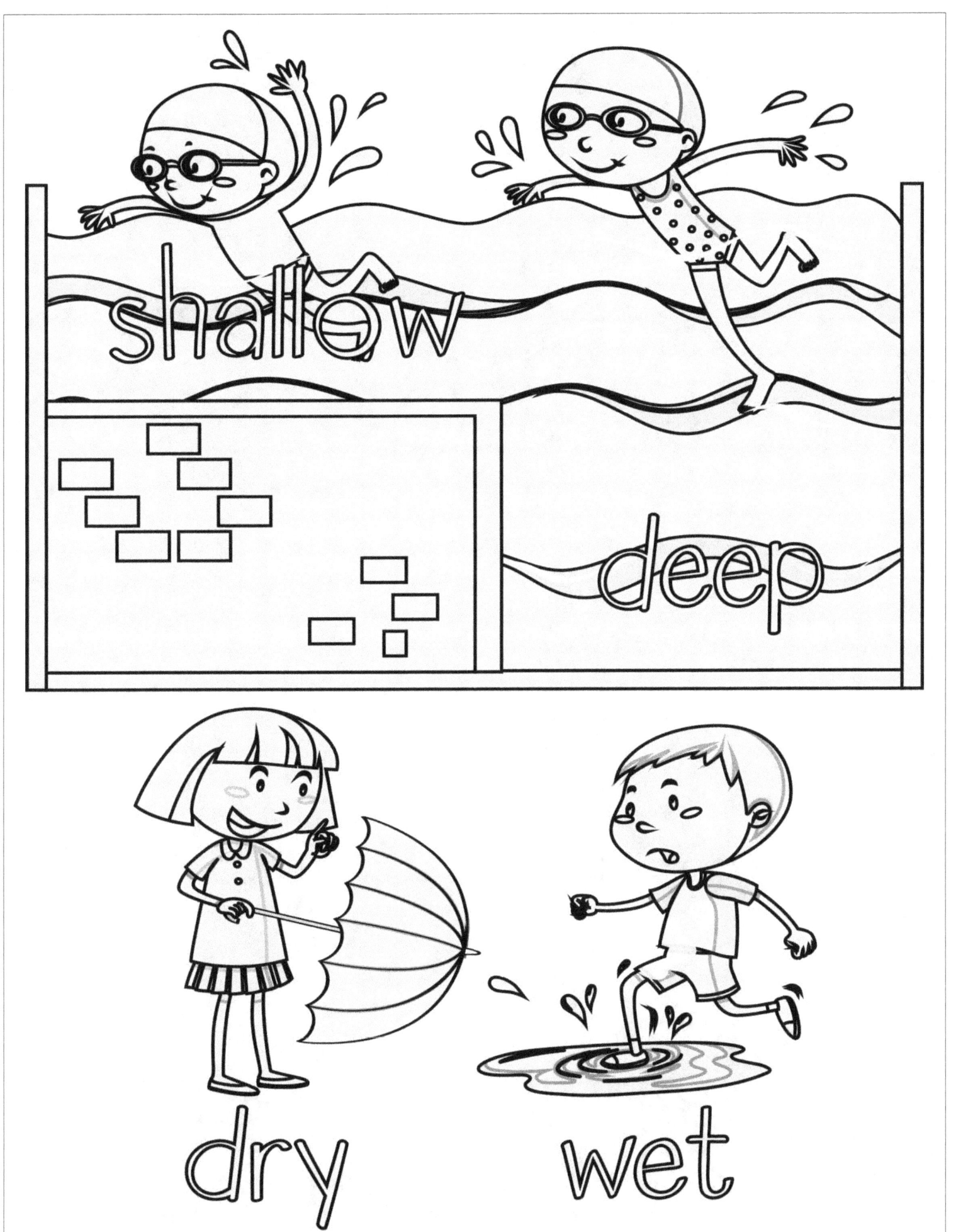

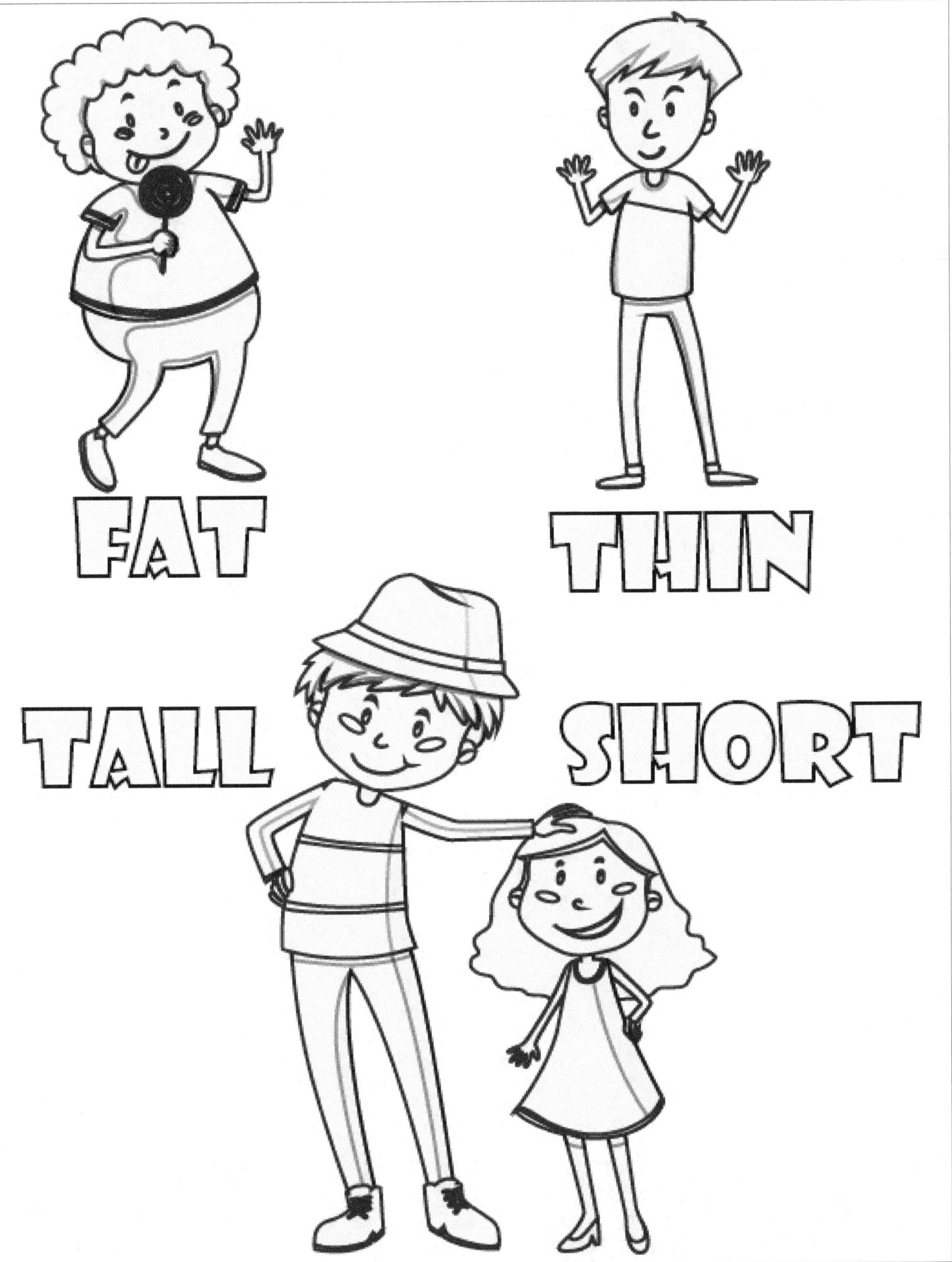

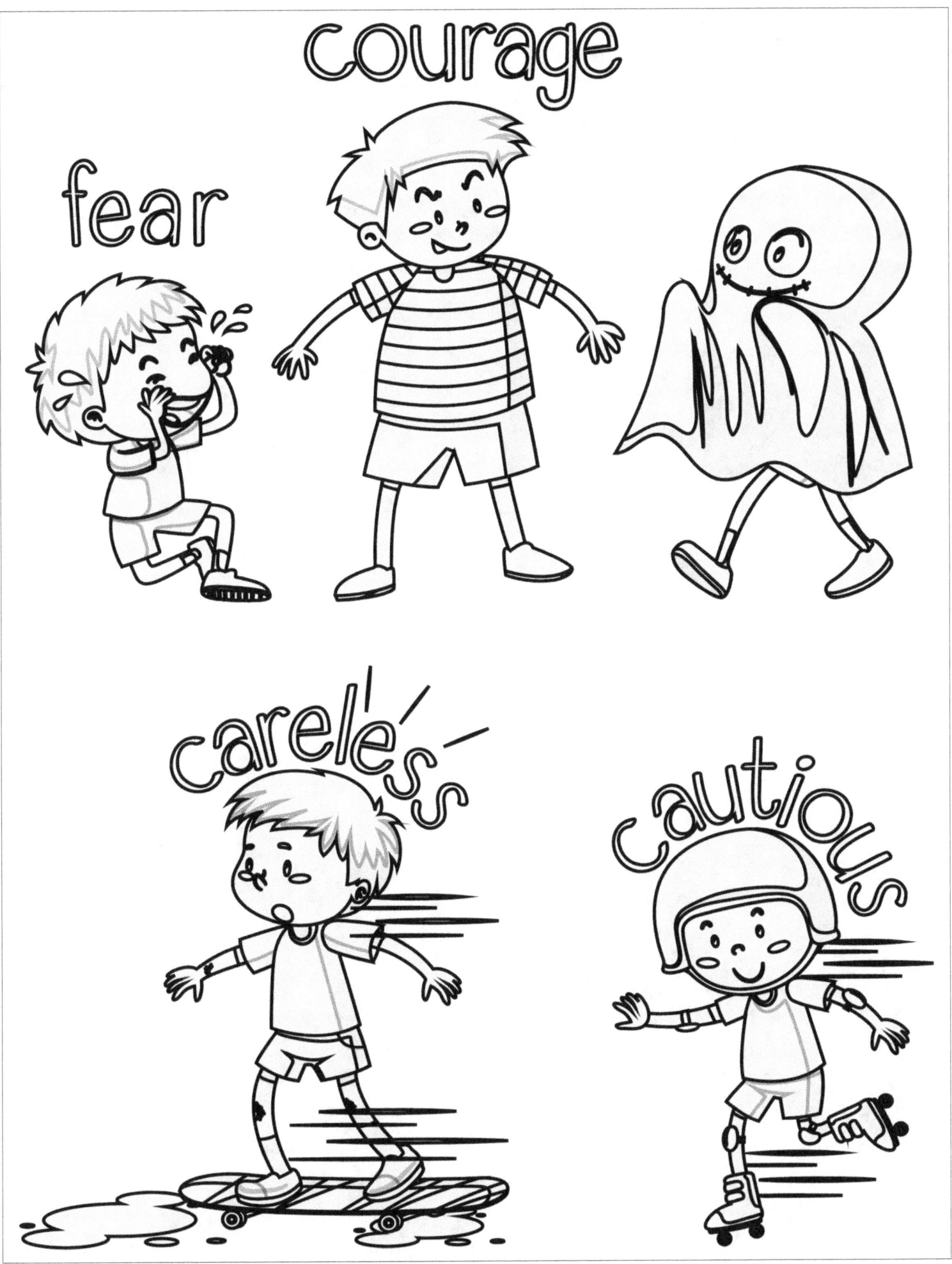

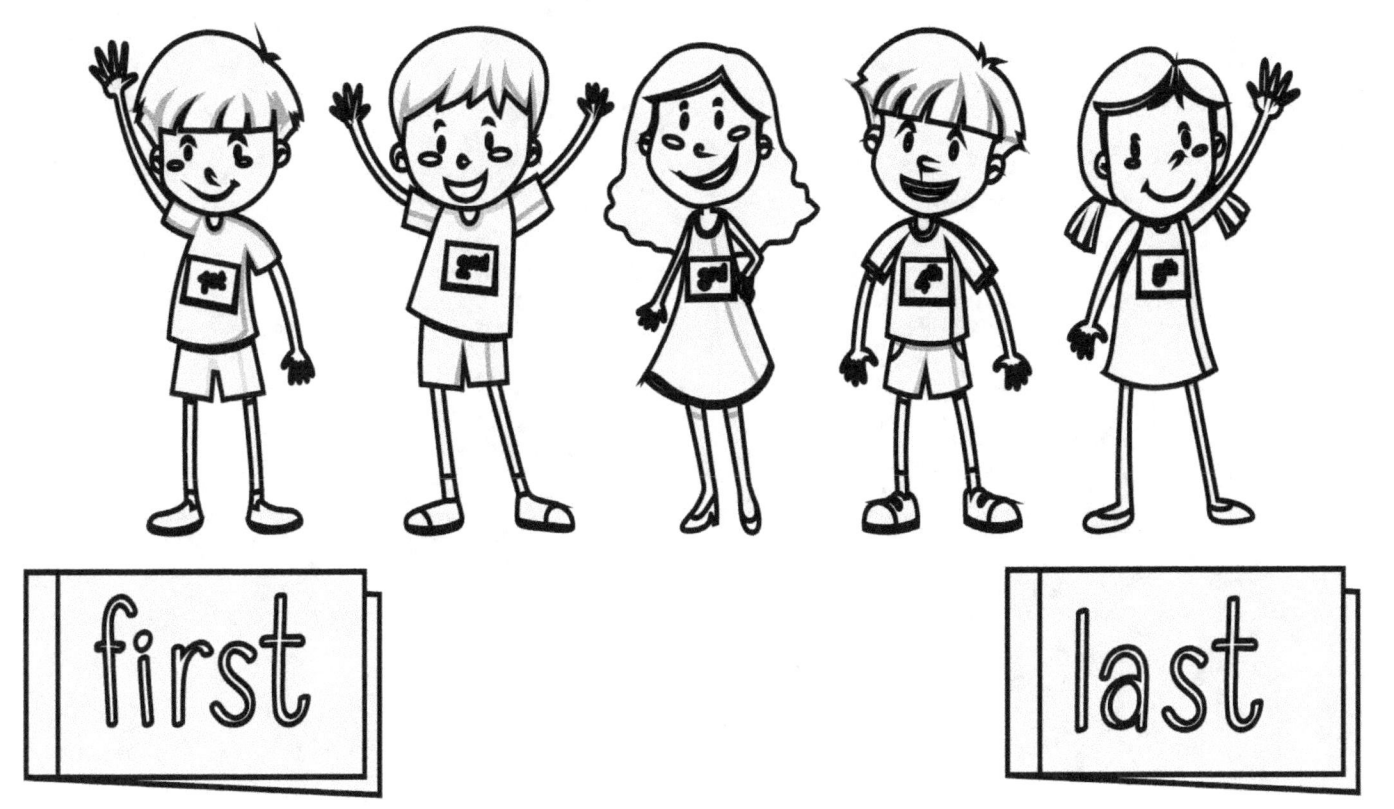

first

last

opaque

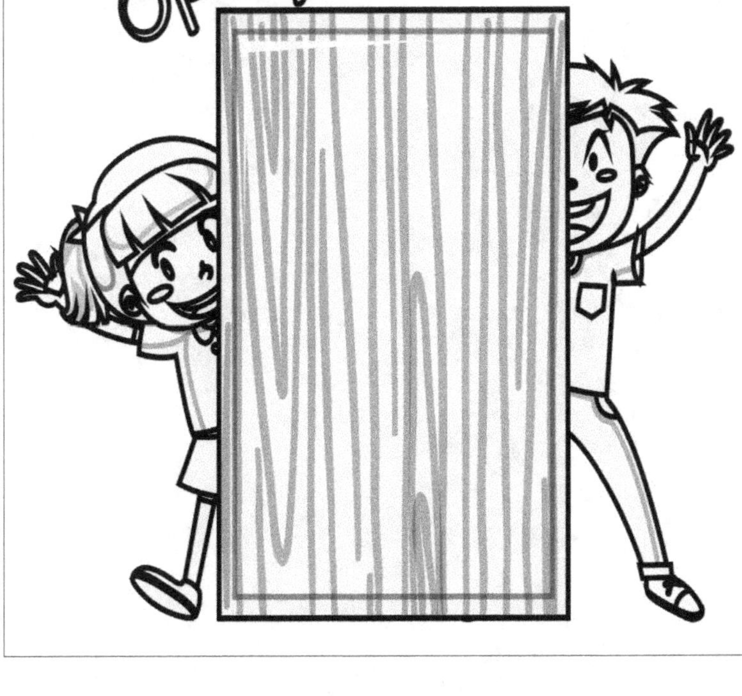

transparent

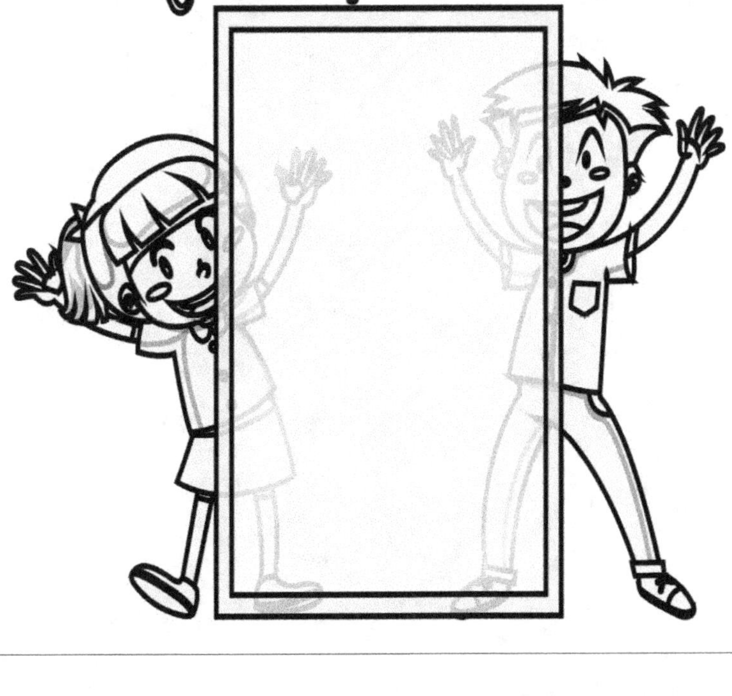

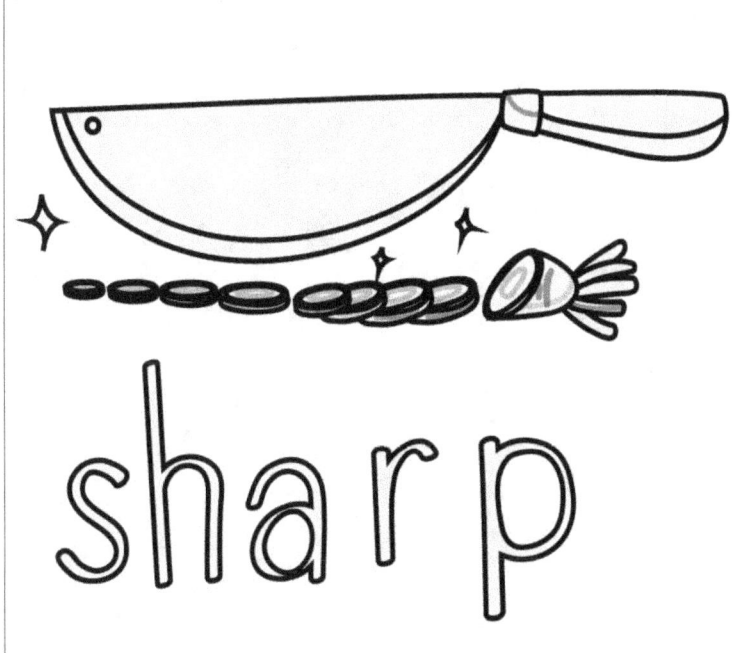

sharp

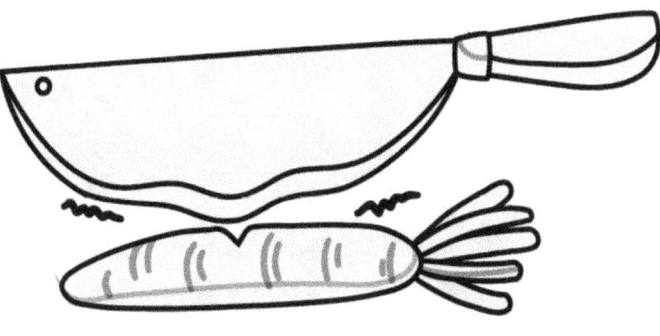

blunt

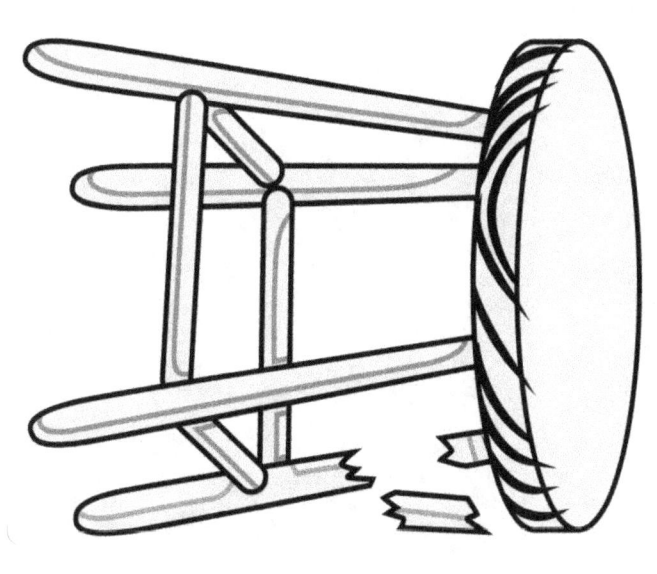

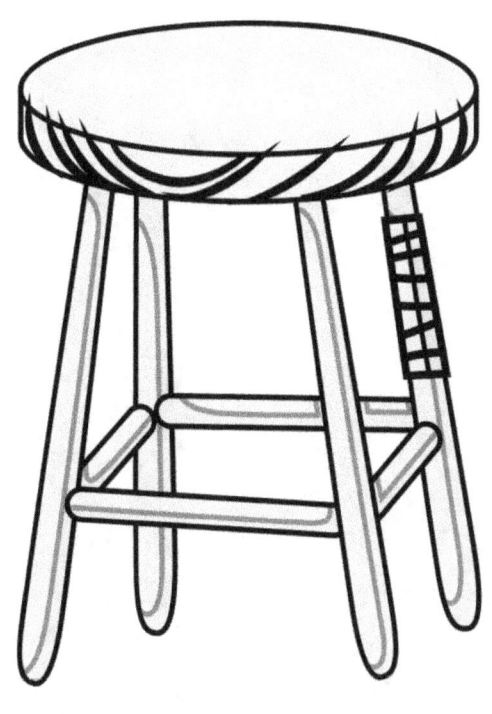

to break   to fix

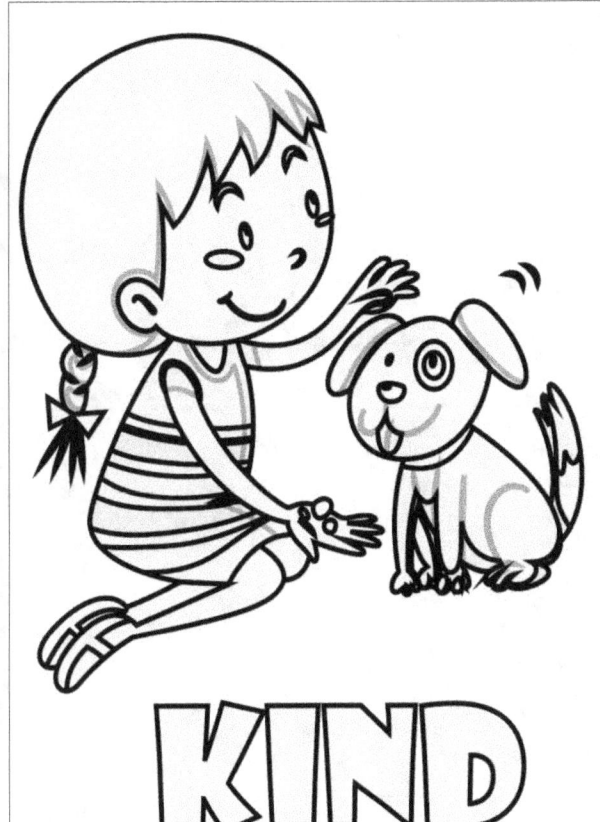
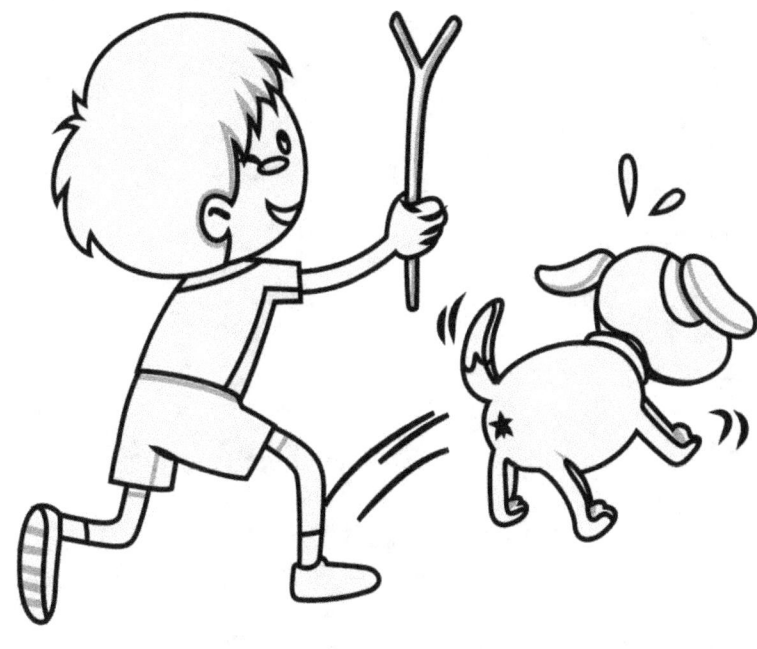

KIND **MEAN**

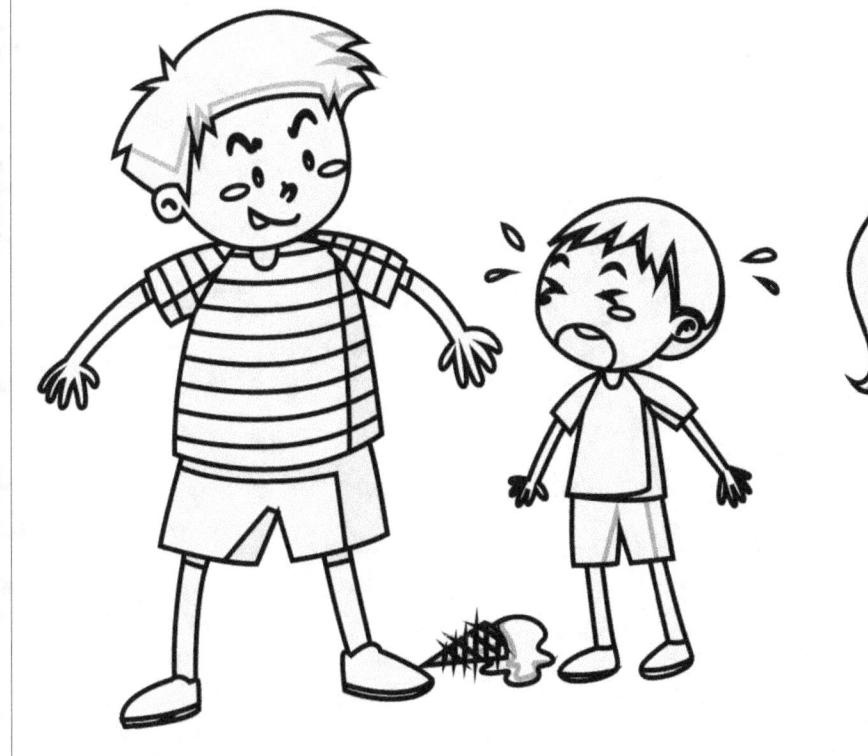

BULLY **FRIENDLY**

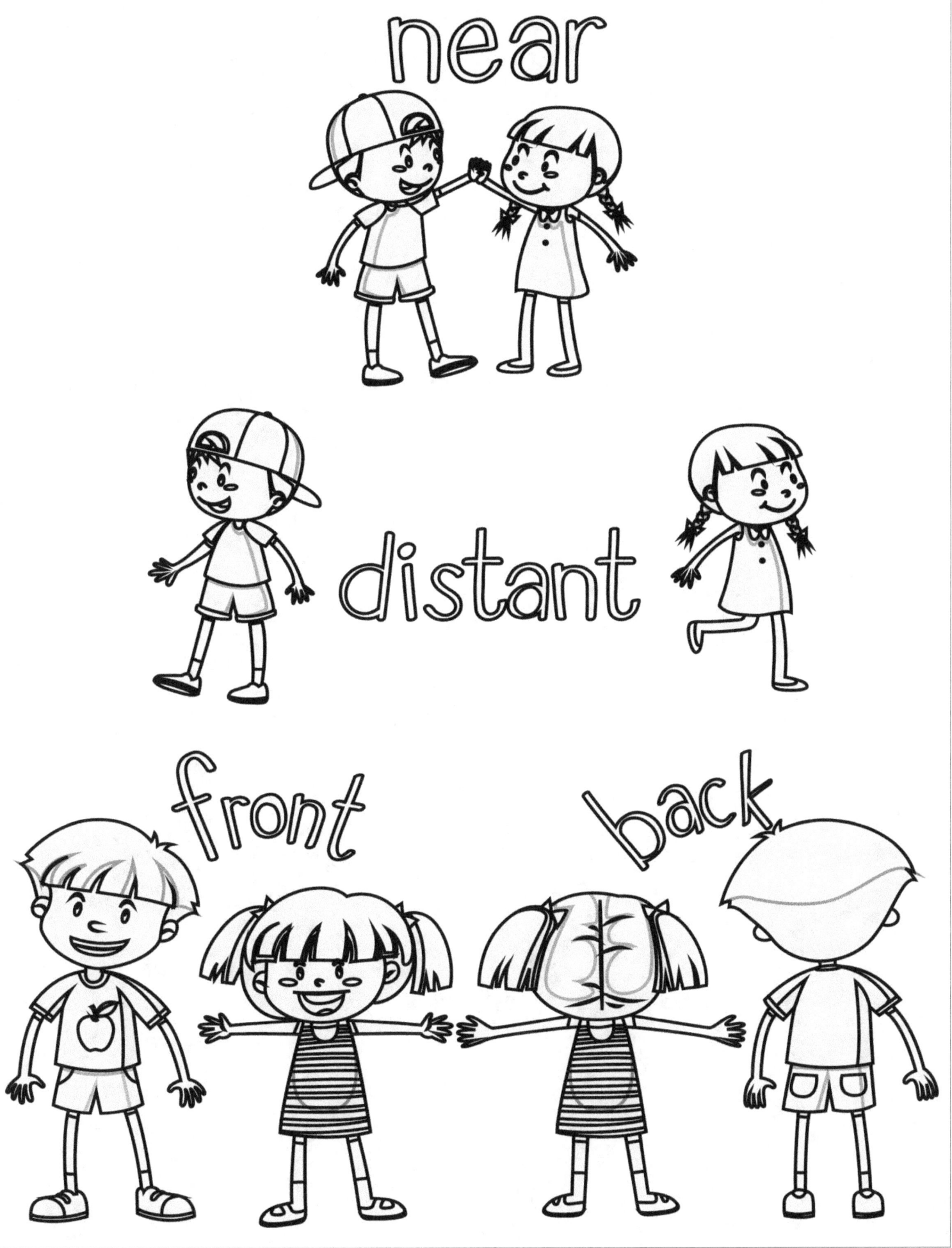

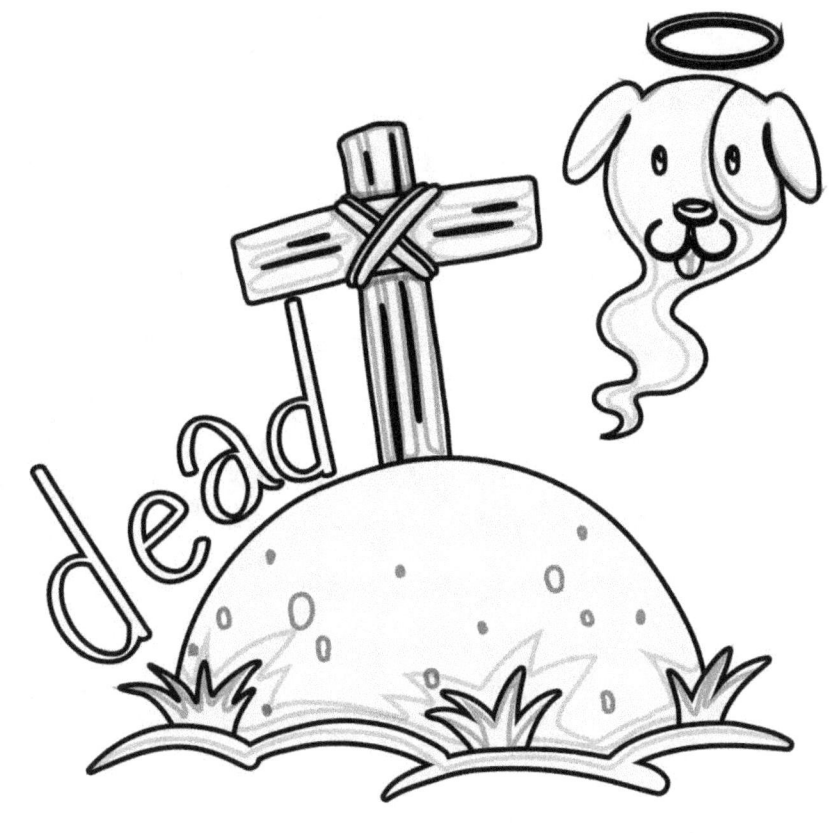
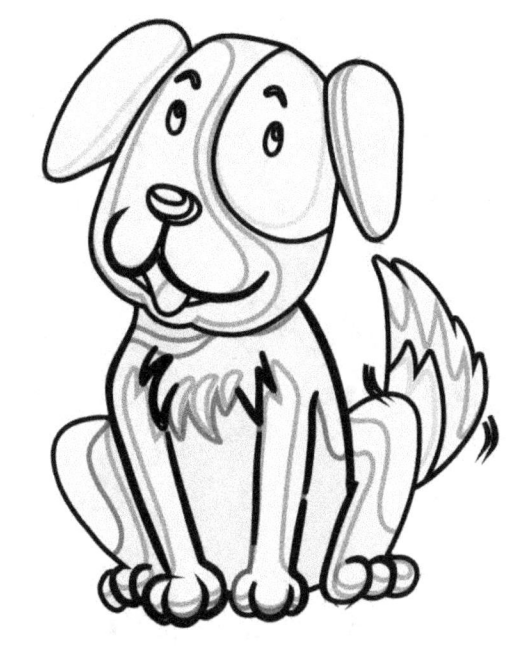

DEAD ## ALIVE

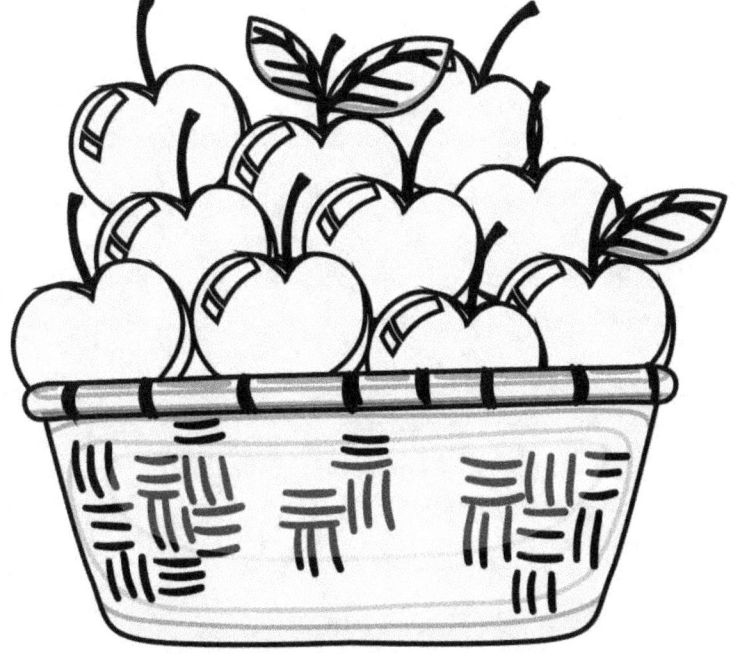
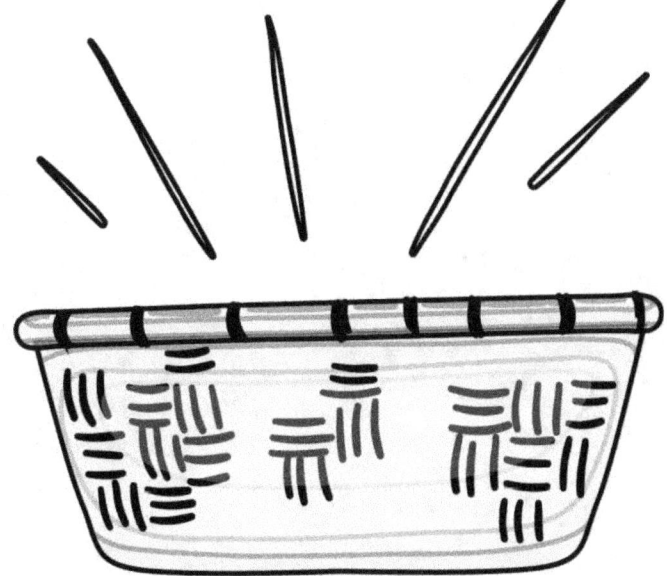

FULL ## EMPTY

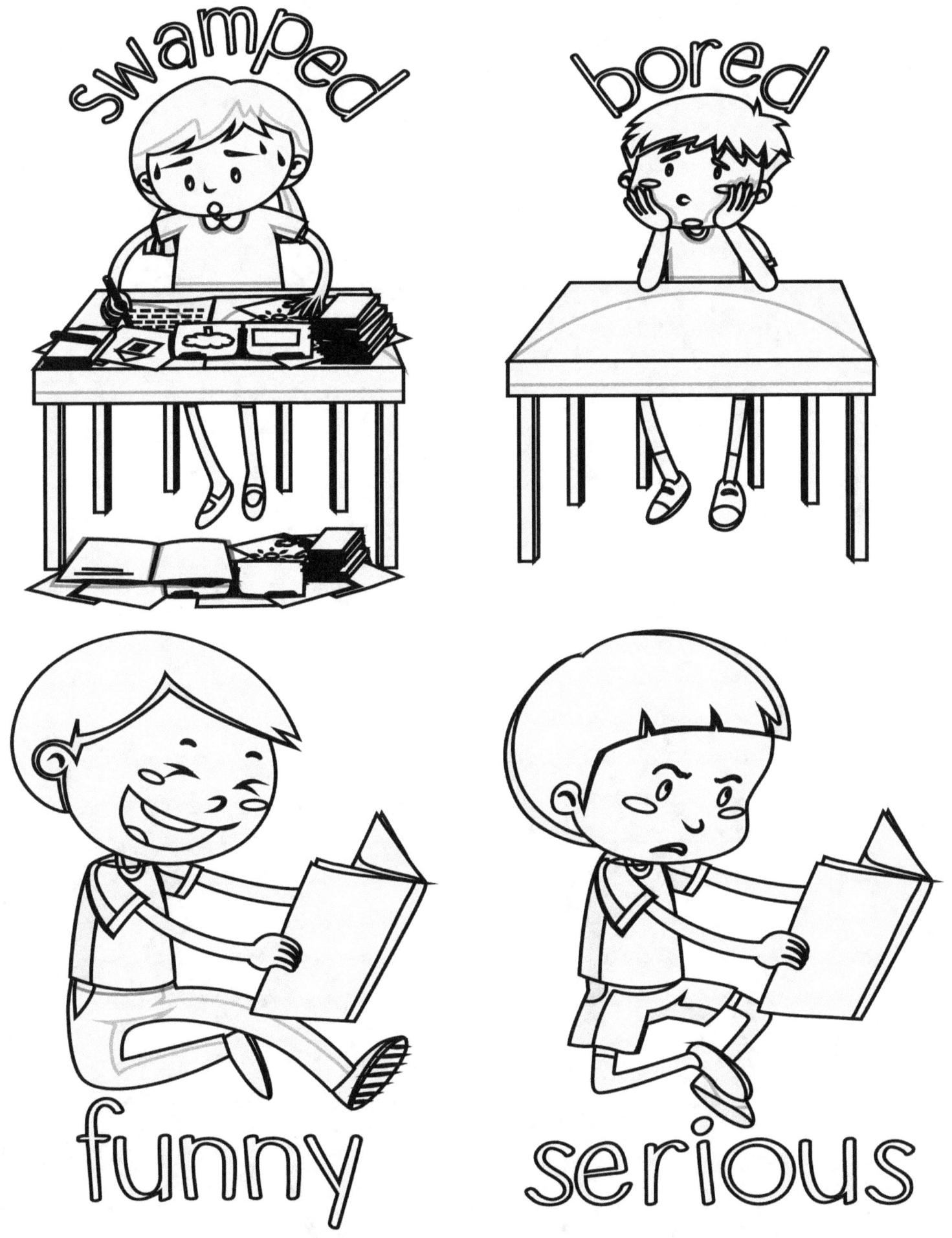

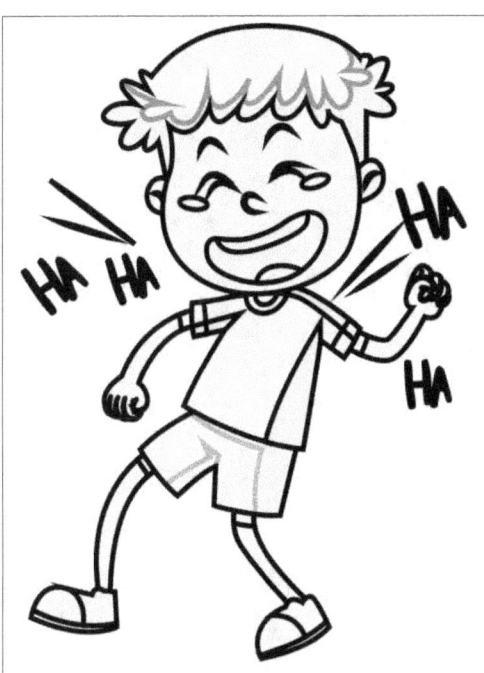 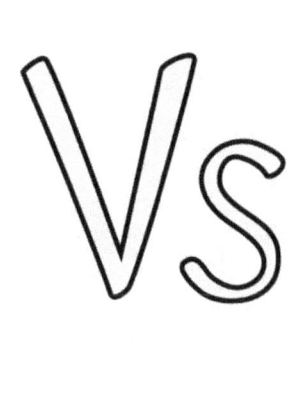 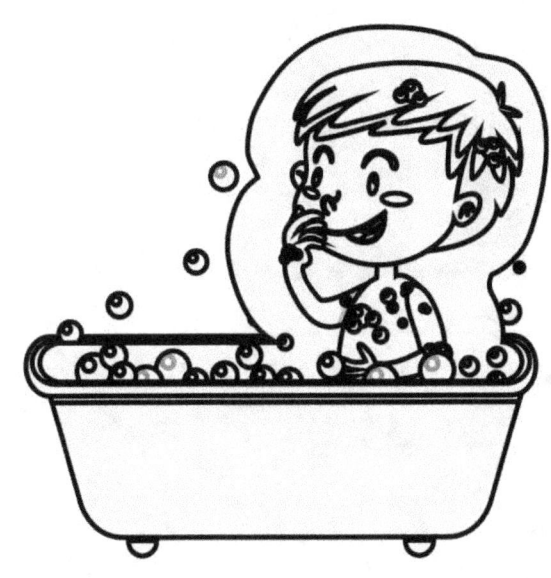

HAVE LAUGH   HAVE A BATH

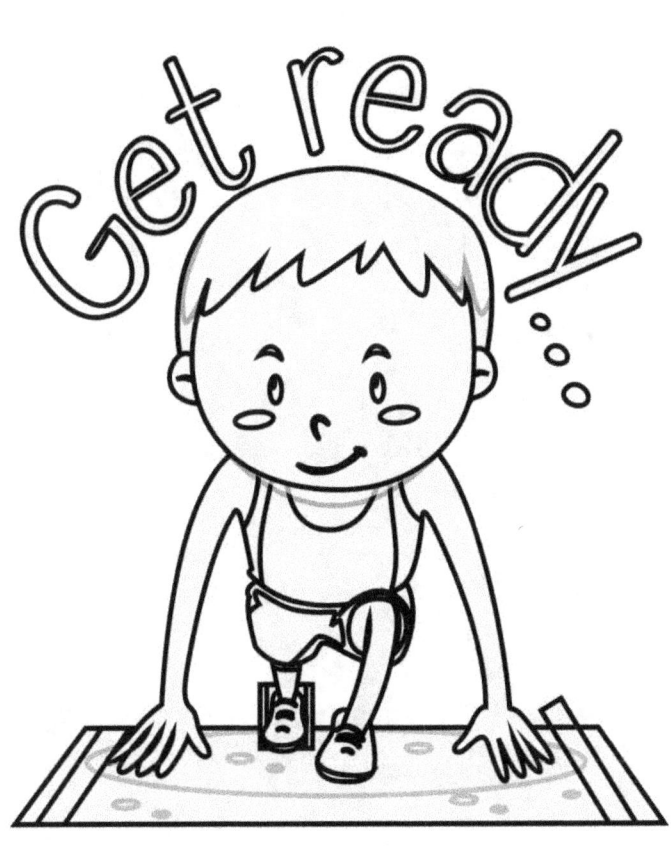 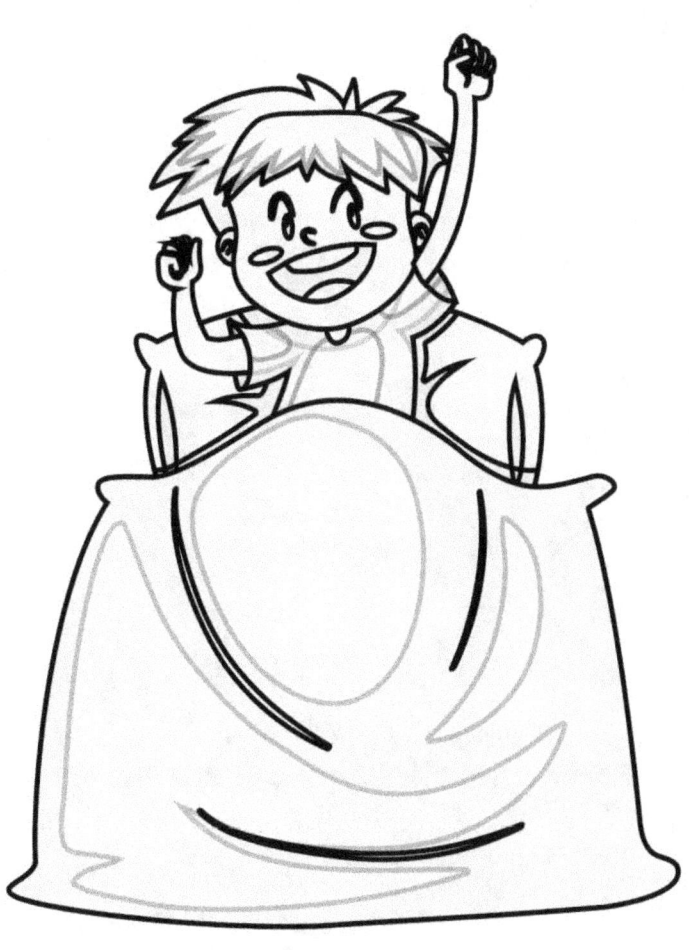

Get up...

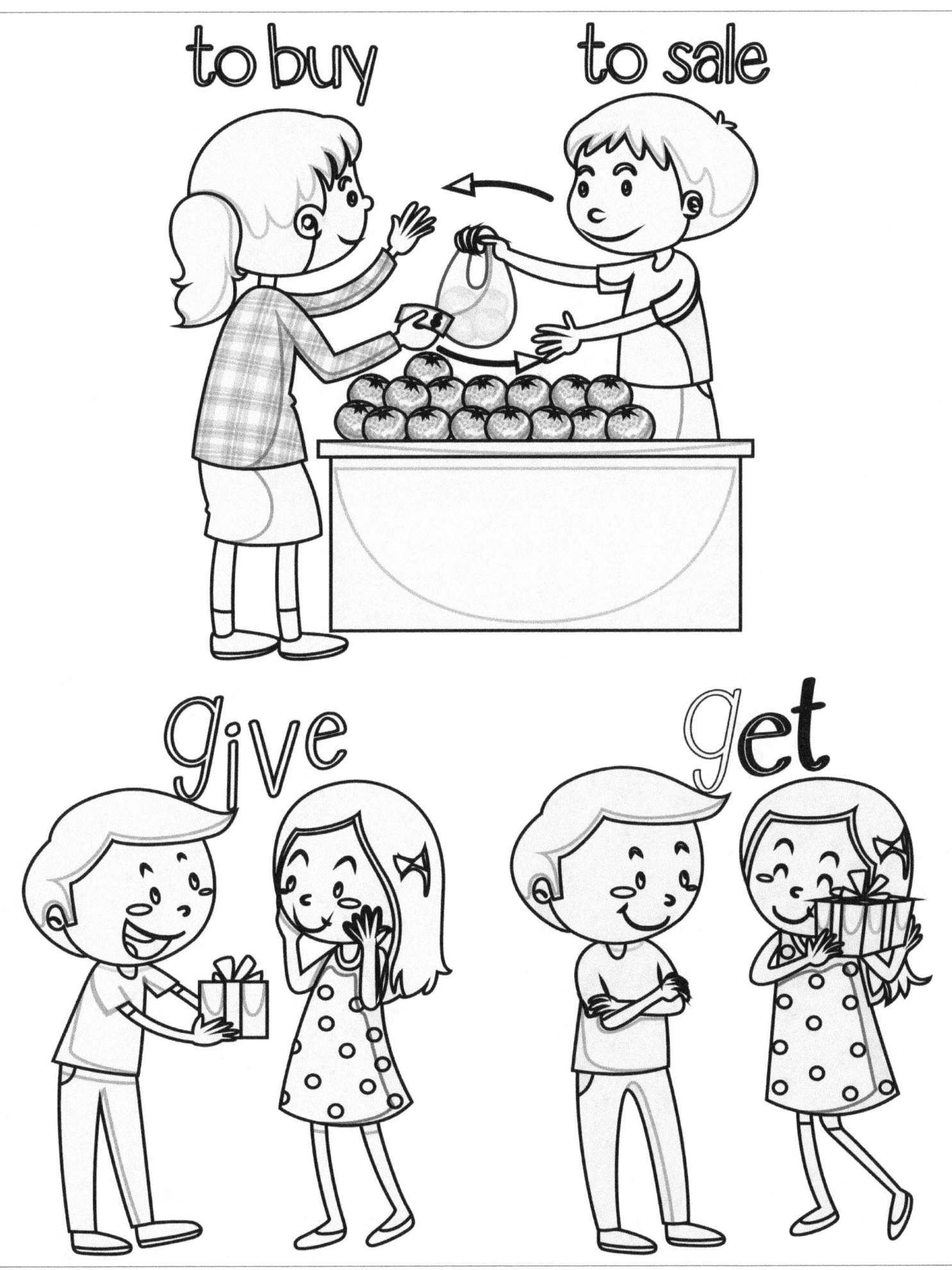

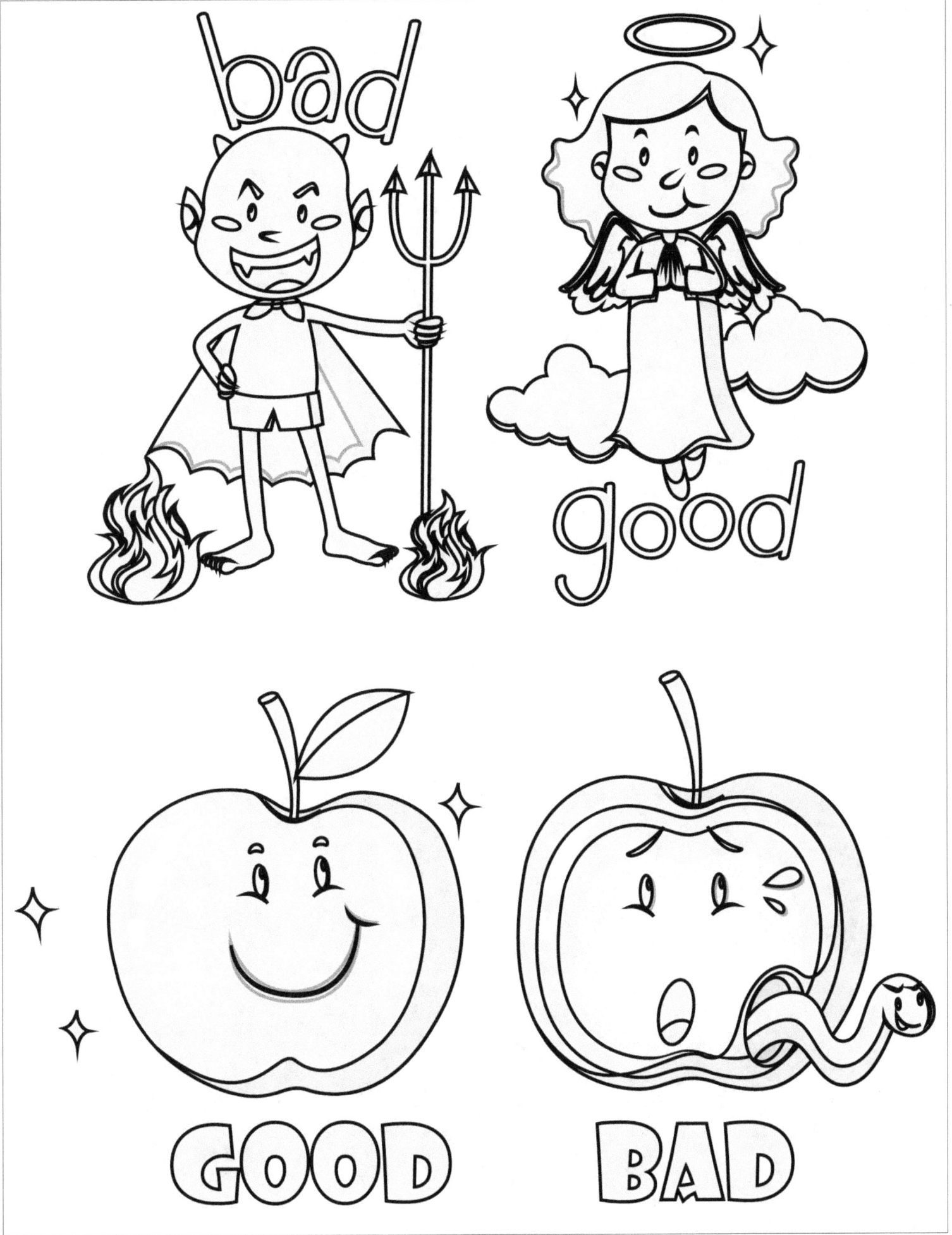

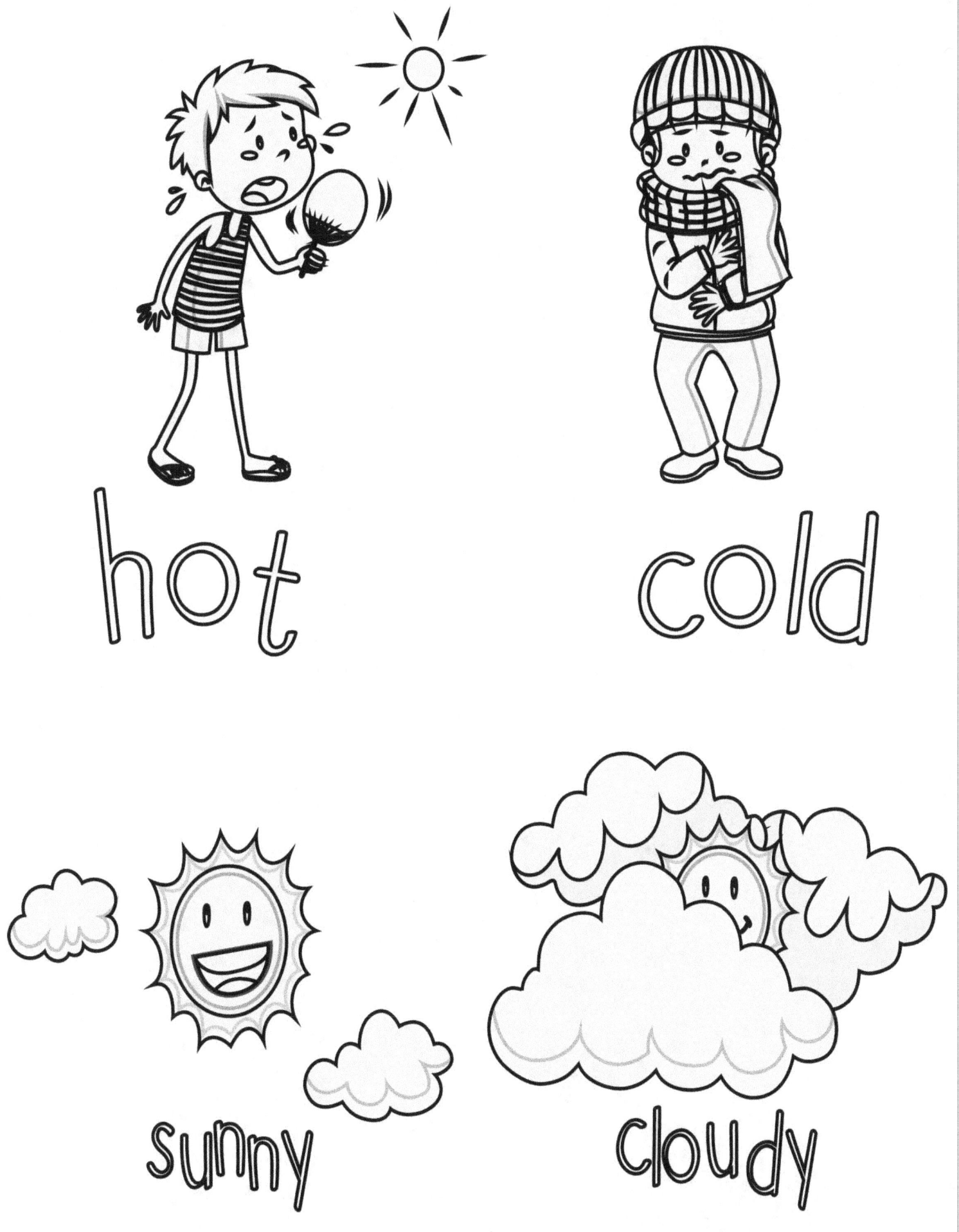

male   female

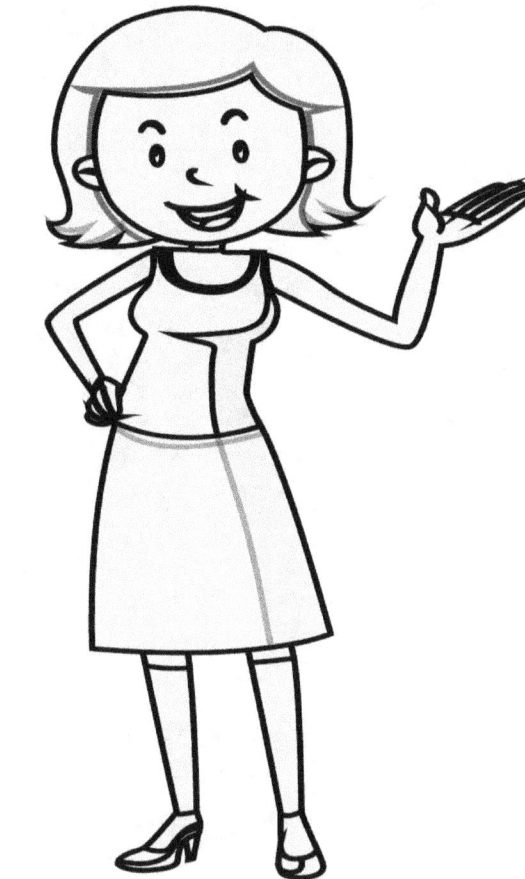

parents

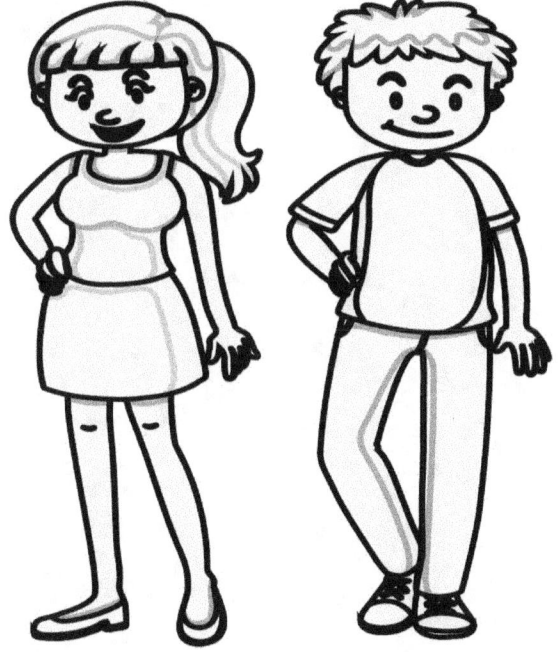

children

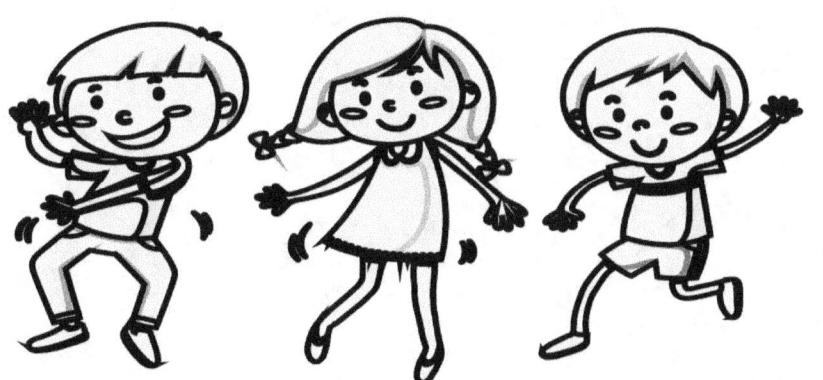

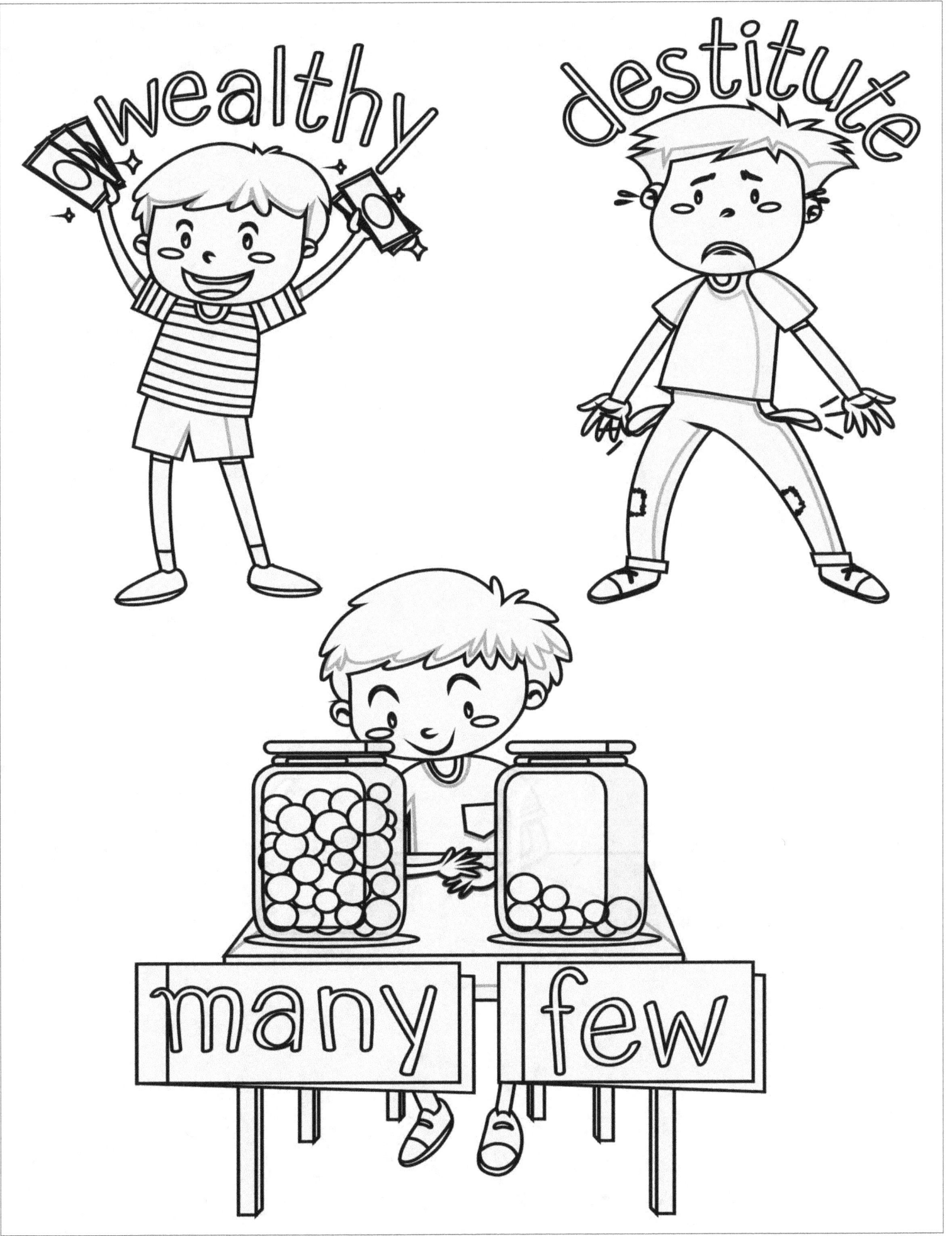

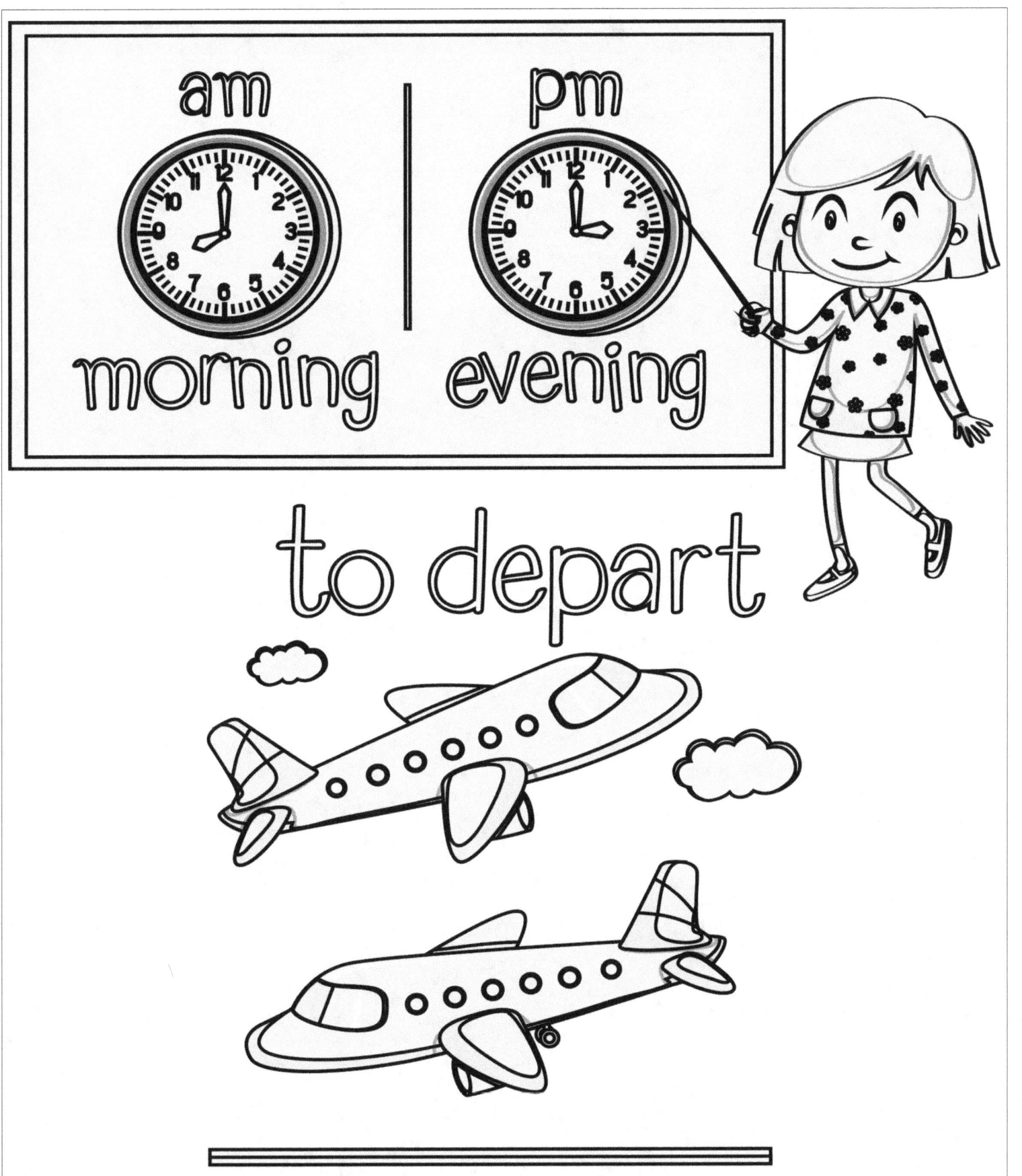

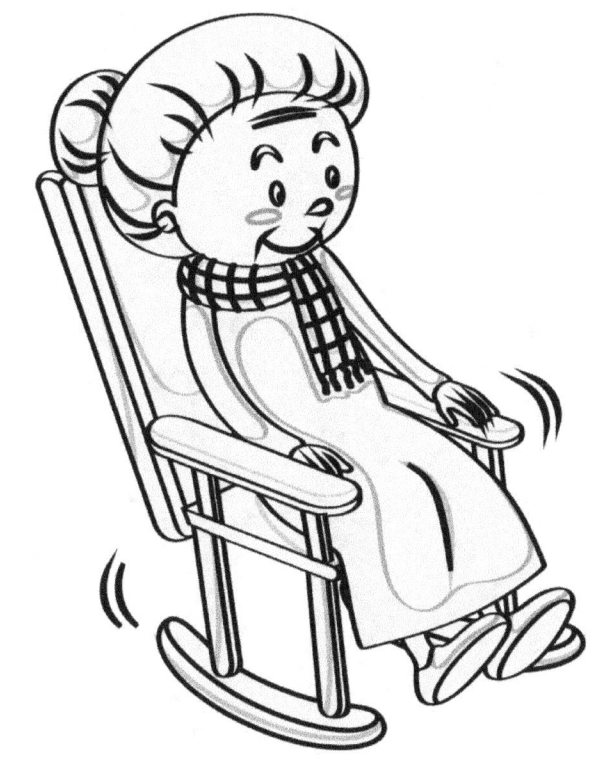
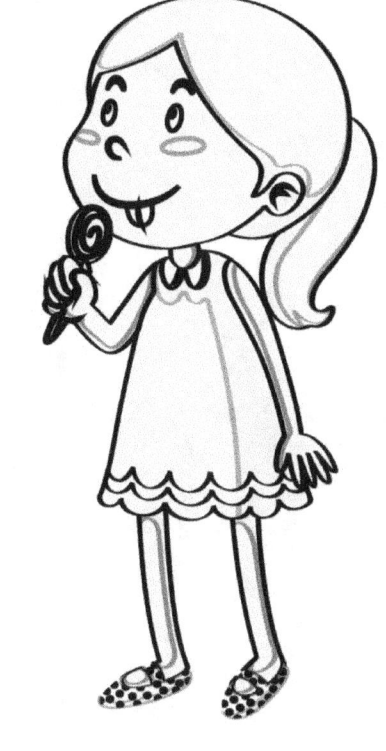

OLD   YOUNG

MOTHER 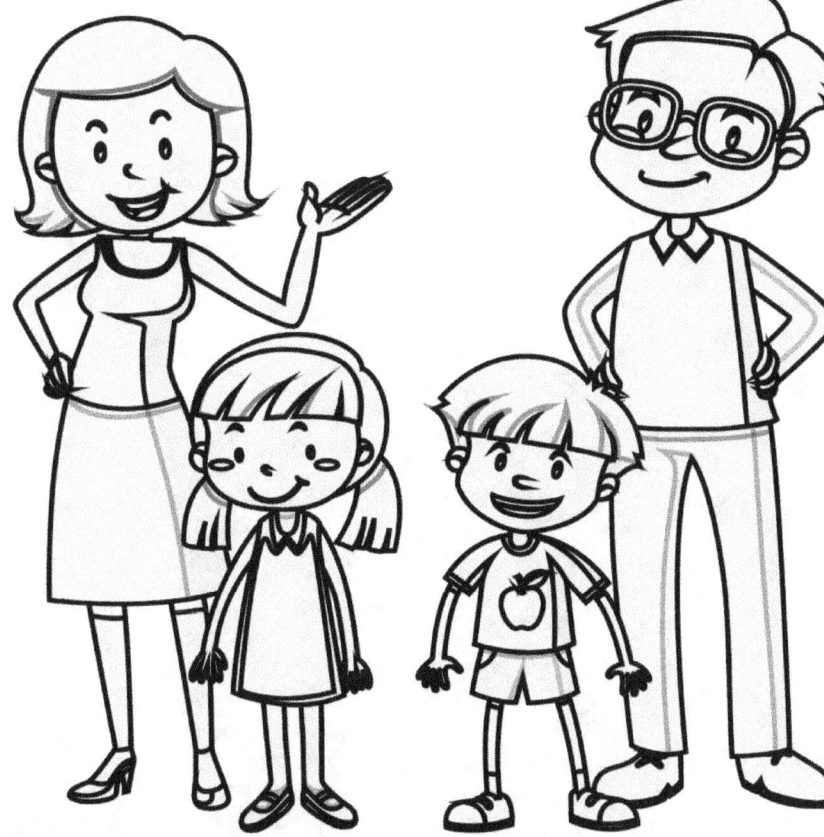 FATHER

DAUGHTER SON

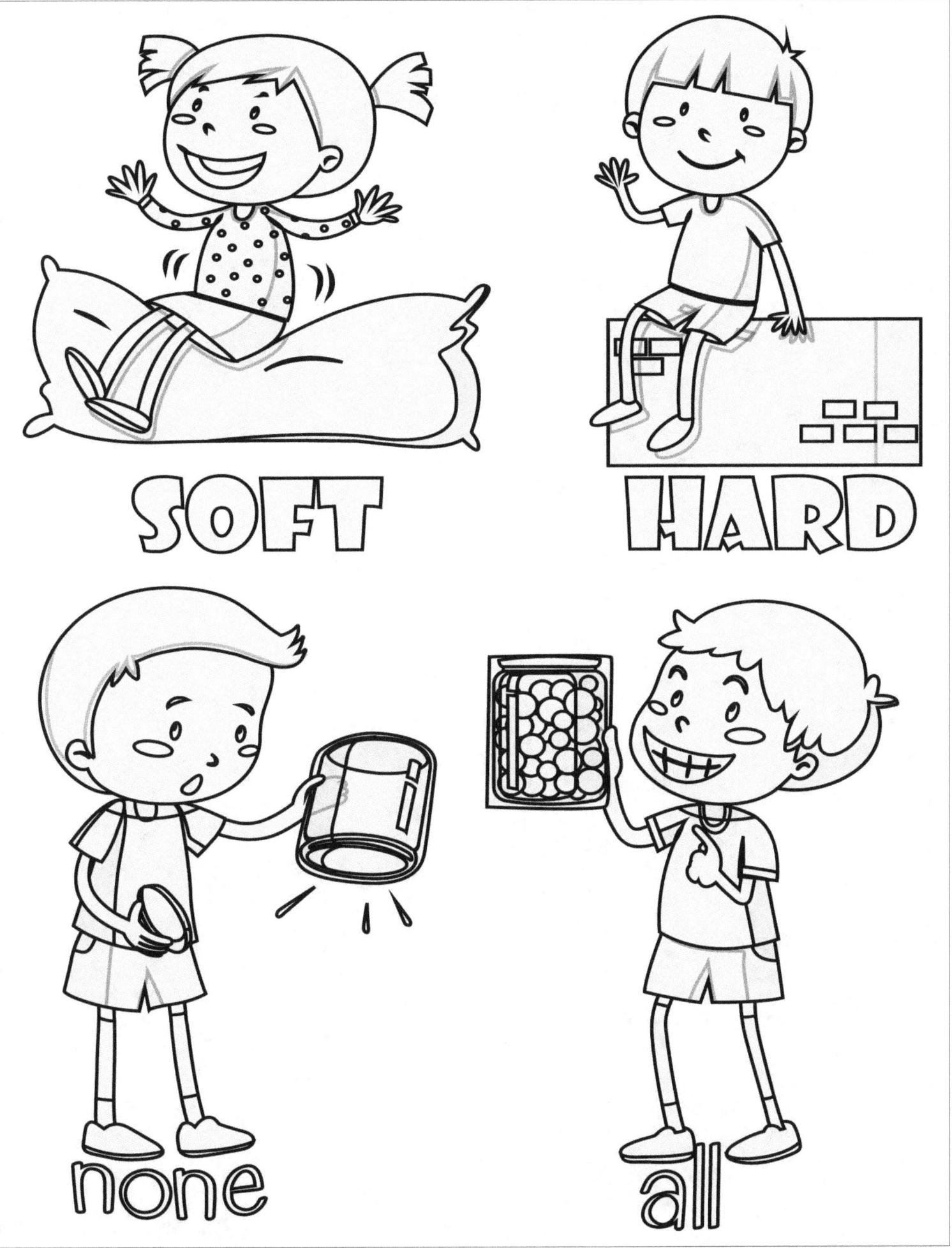

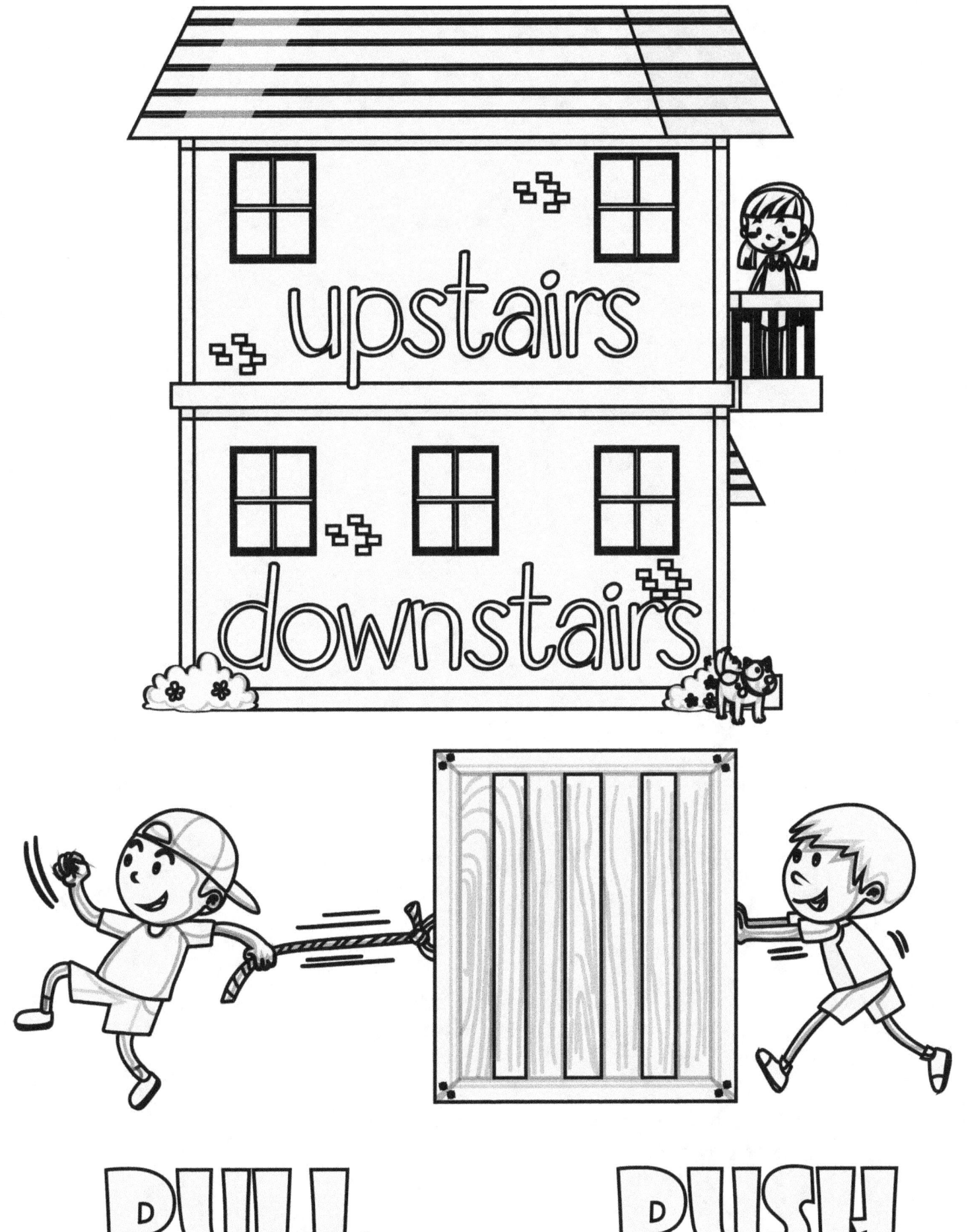

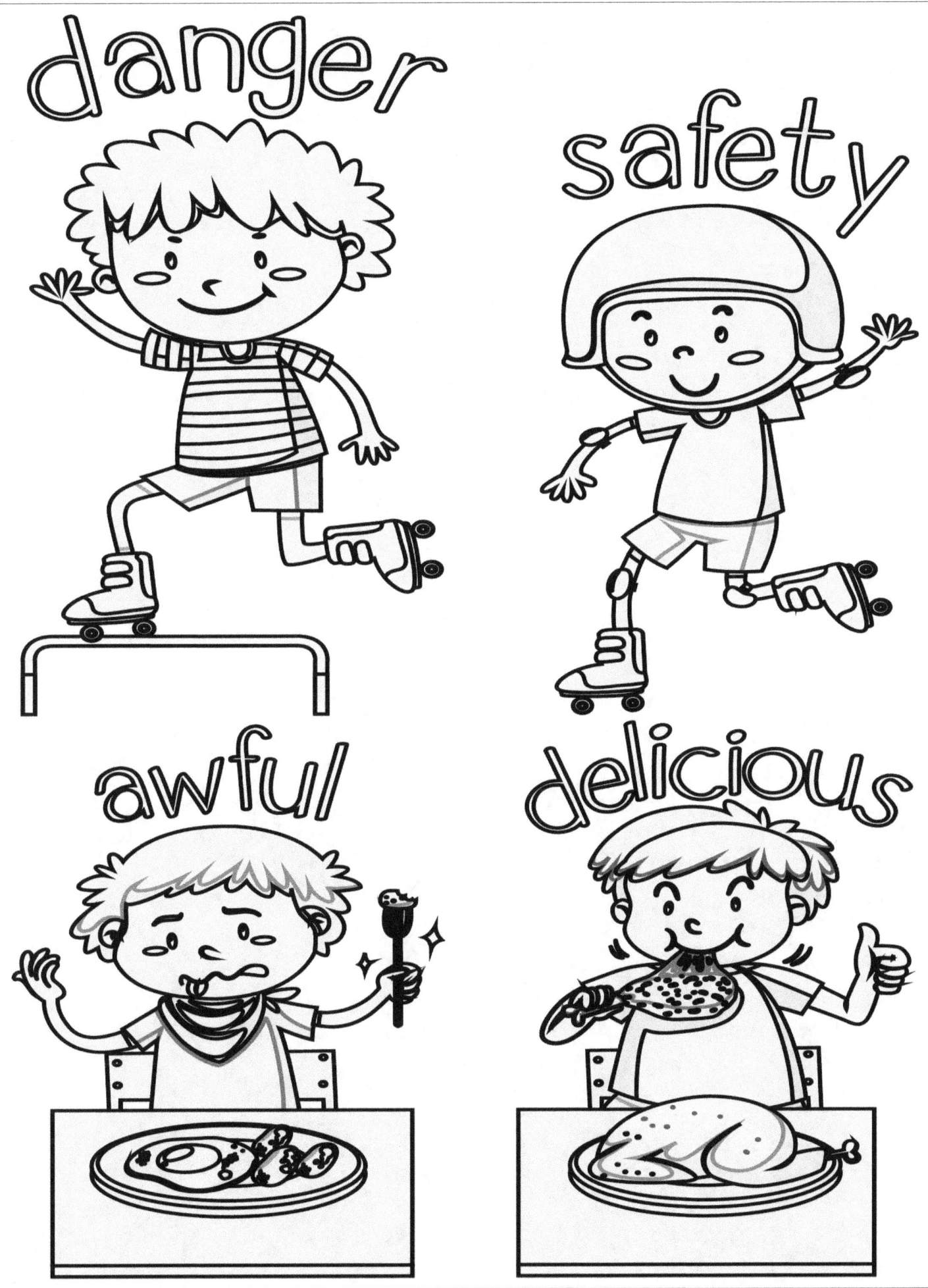

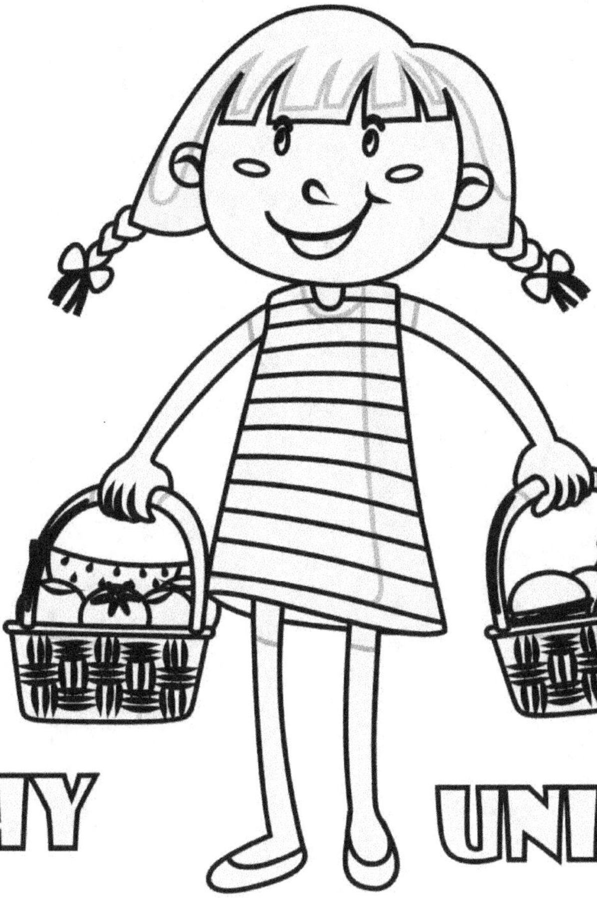

HEALTHY   UNHEALTHY

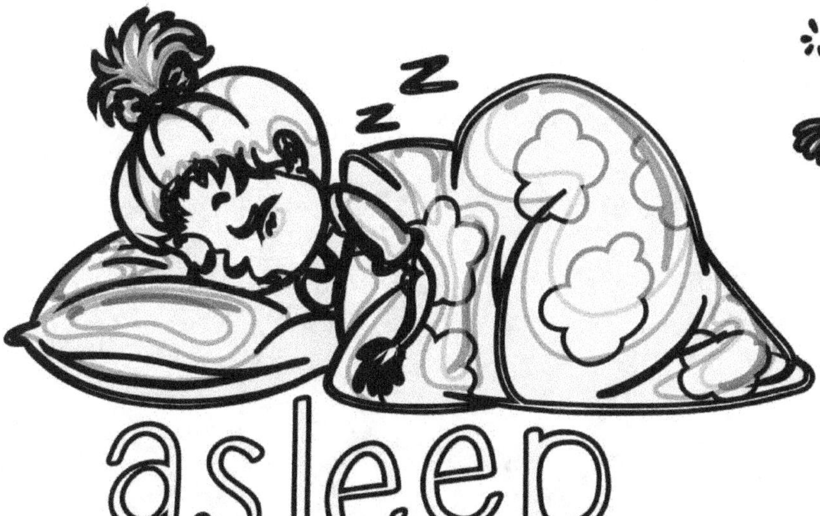

asleep 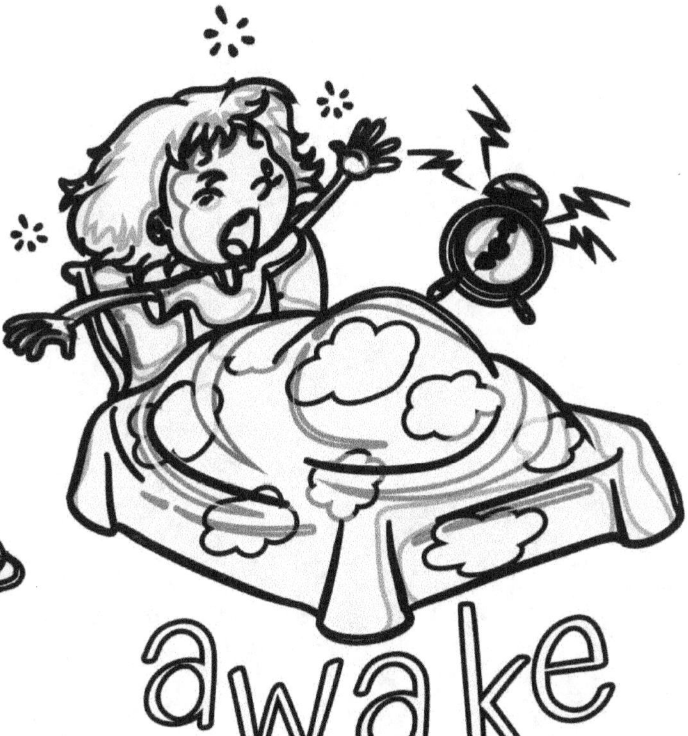   awake

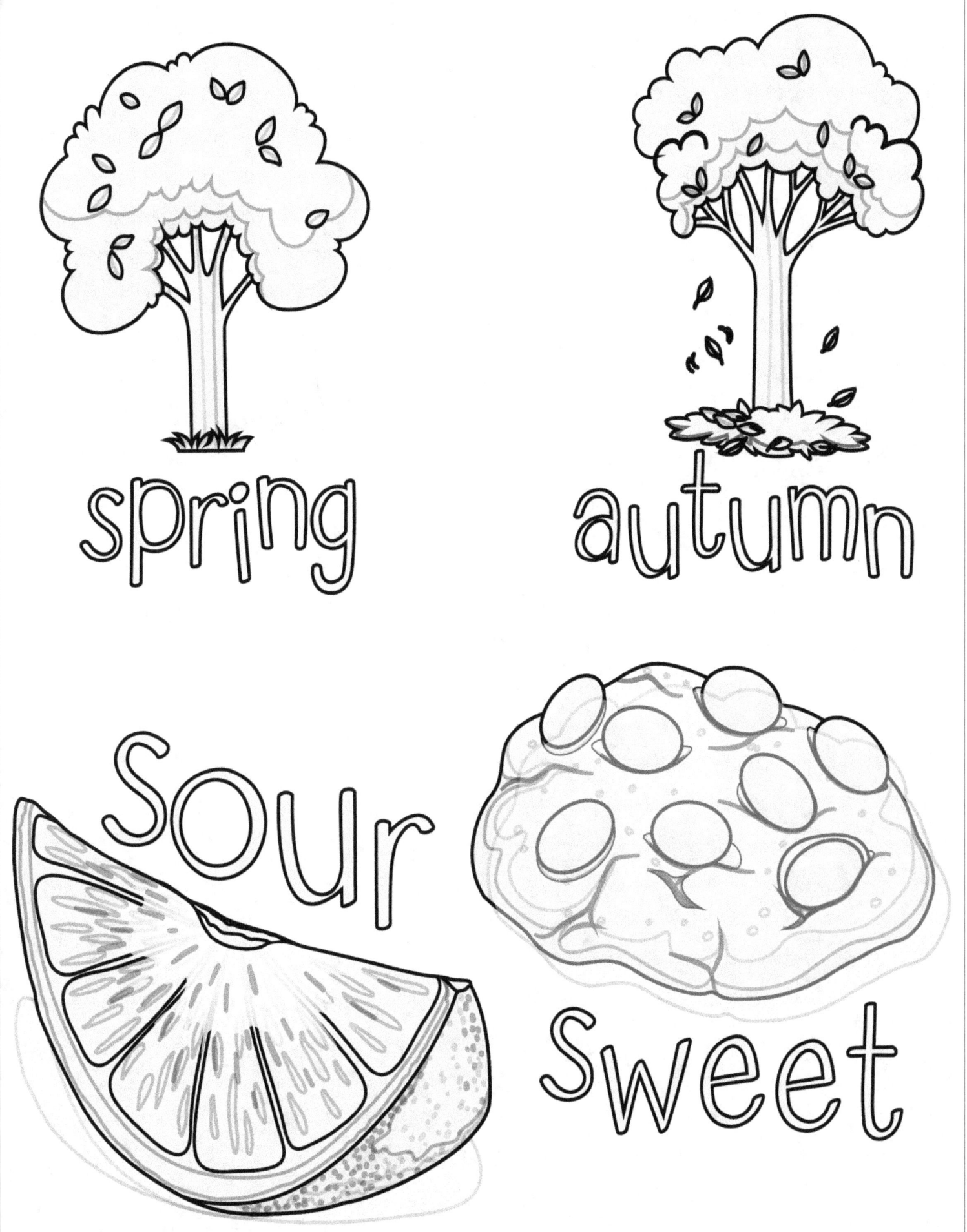

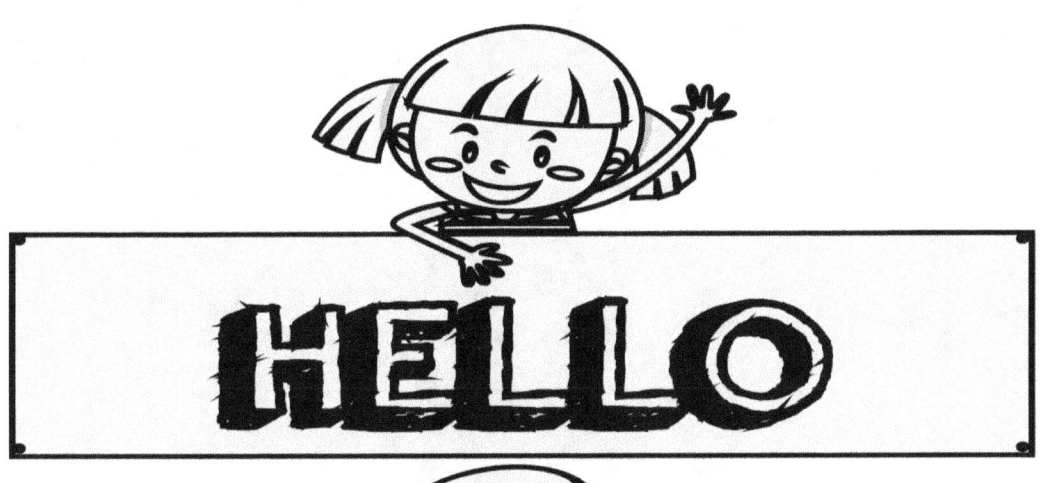

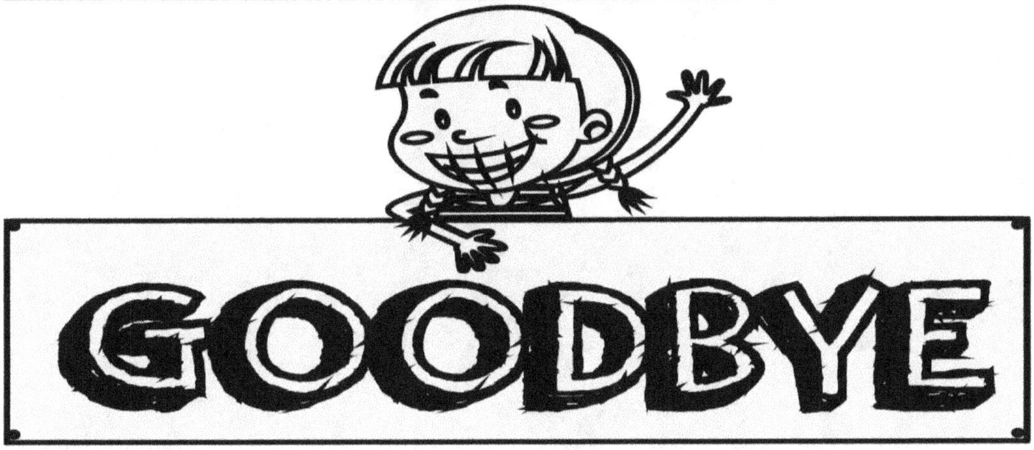

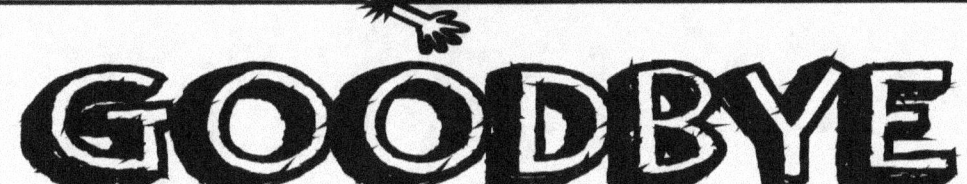

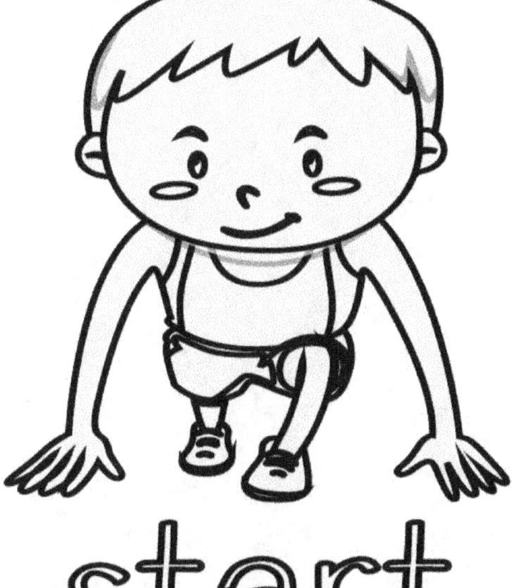

start 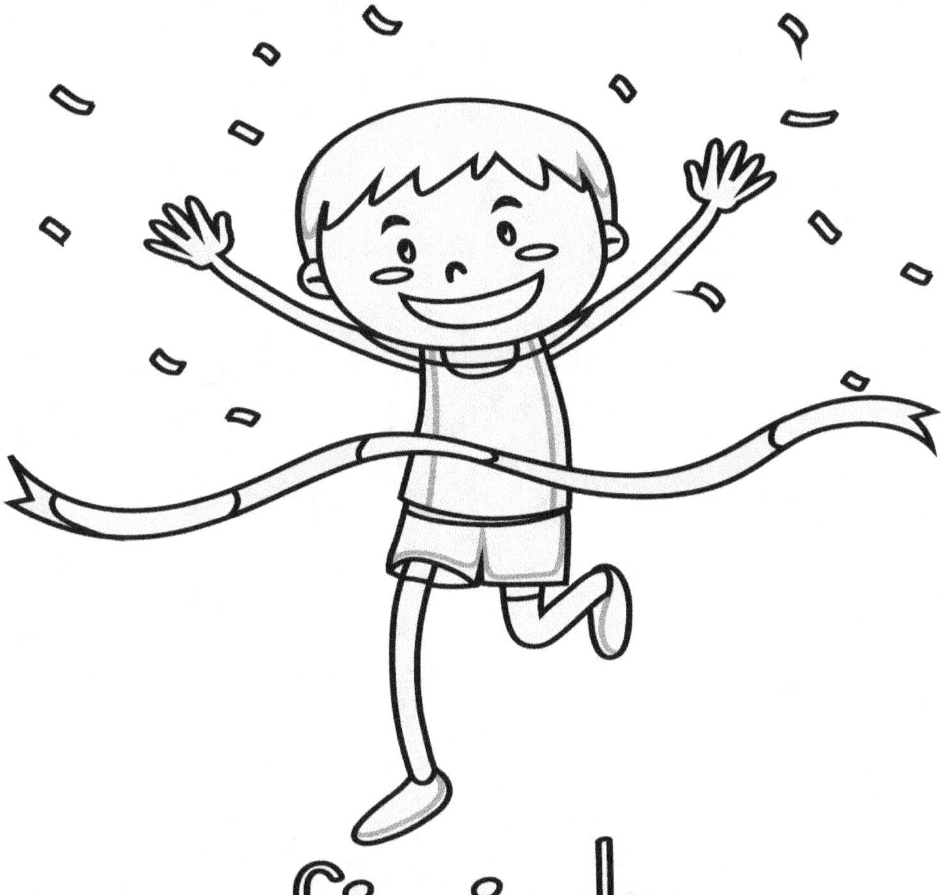 finish

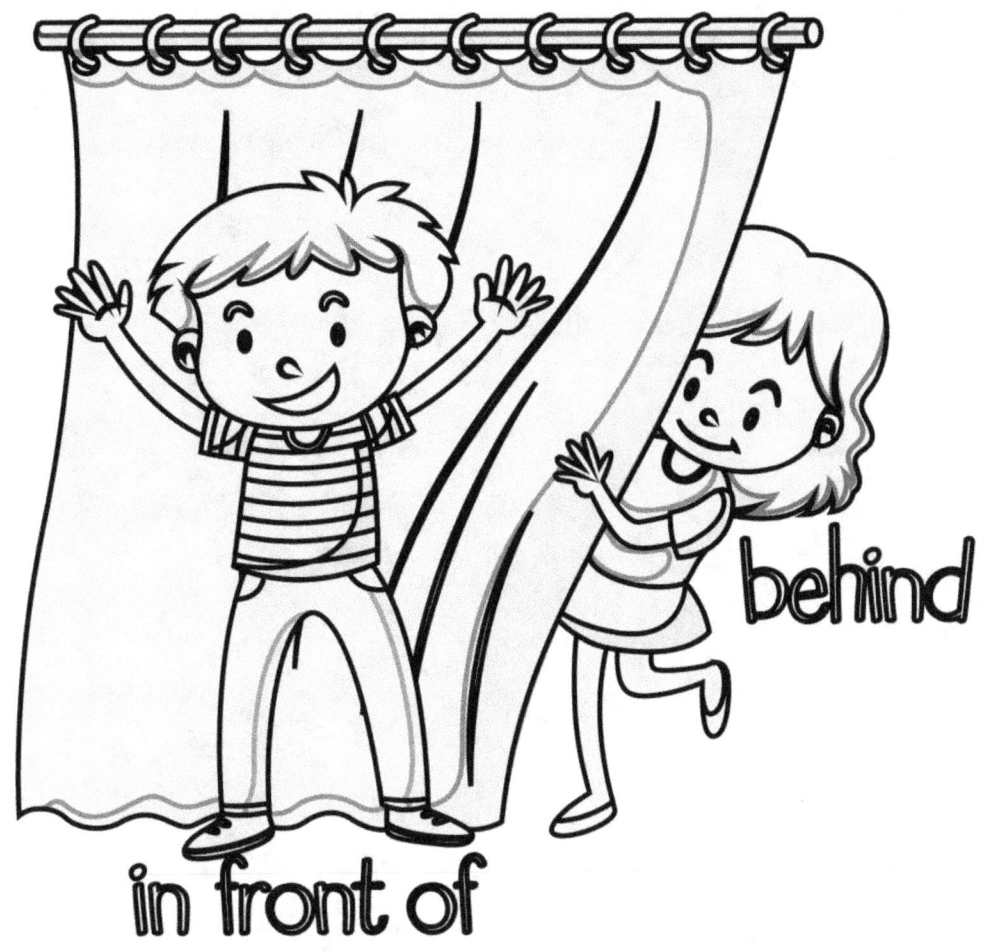

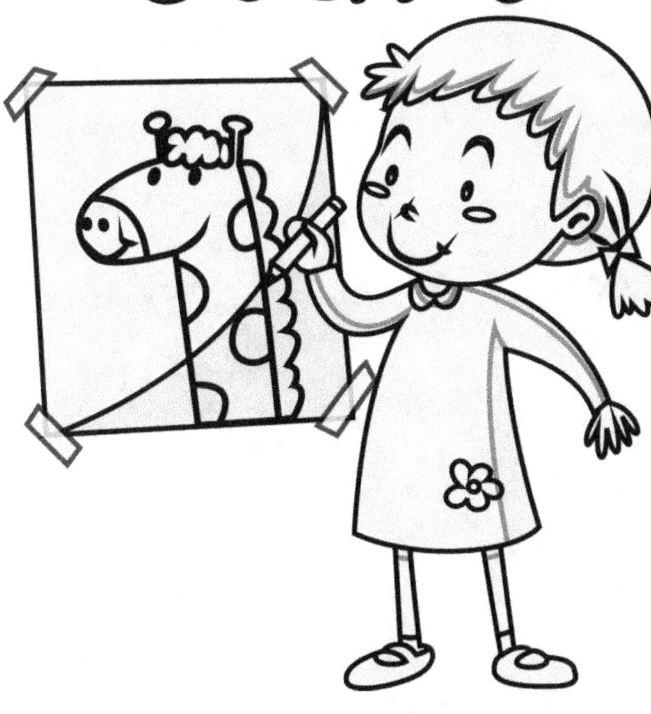

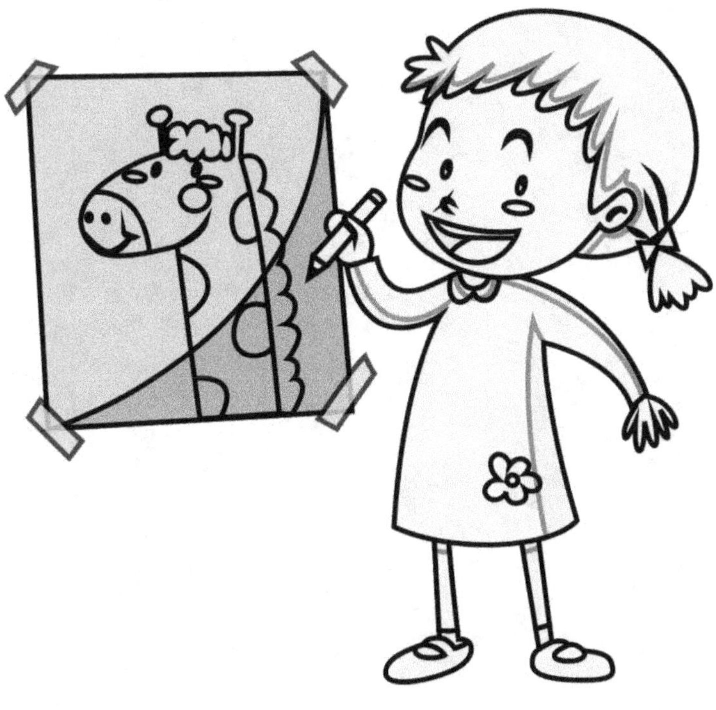

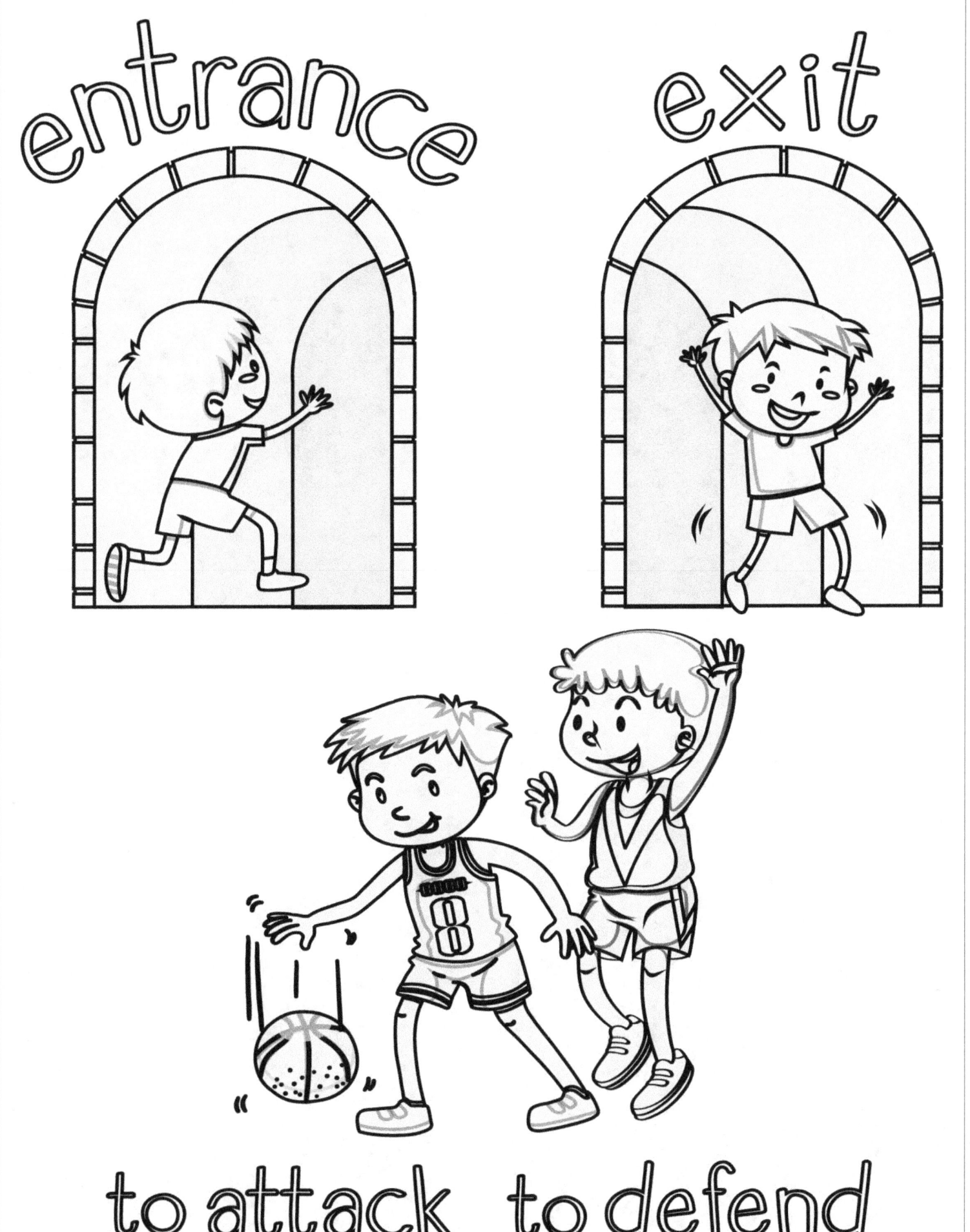

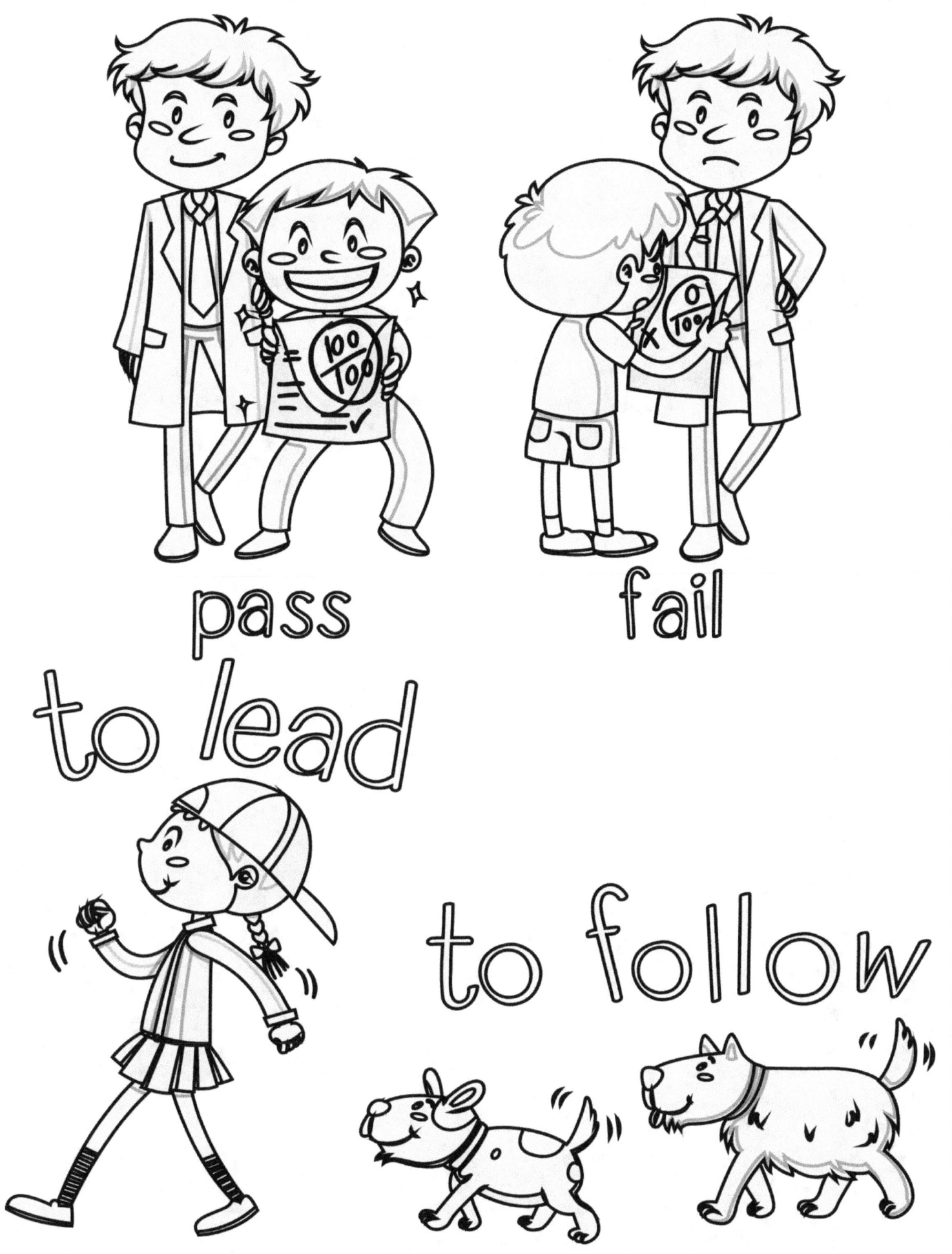

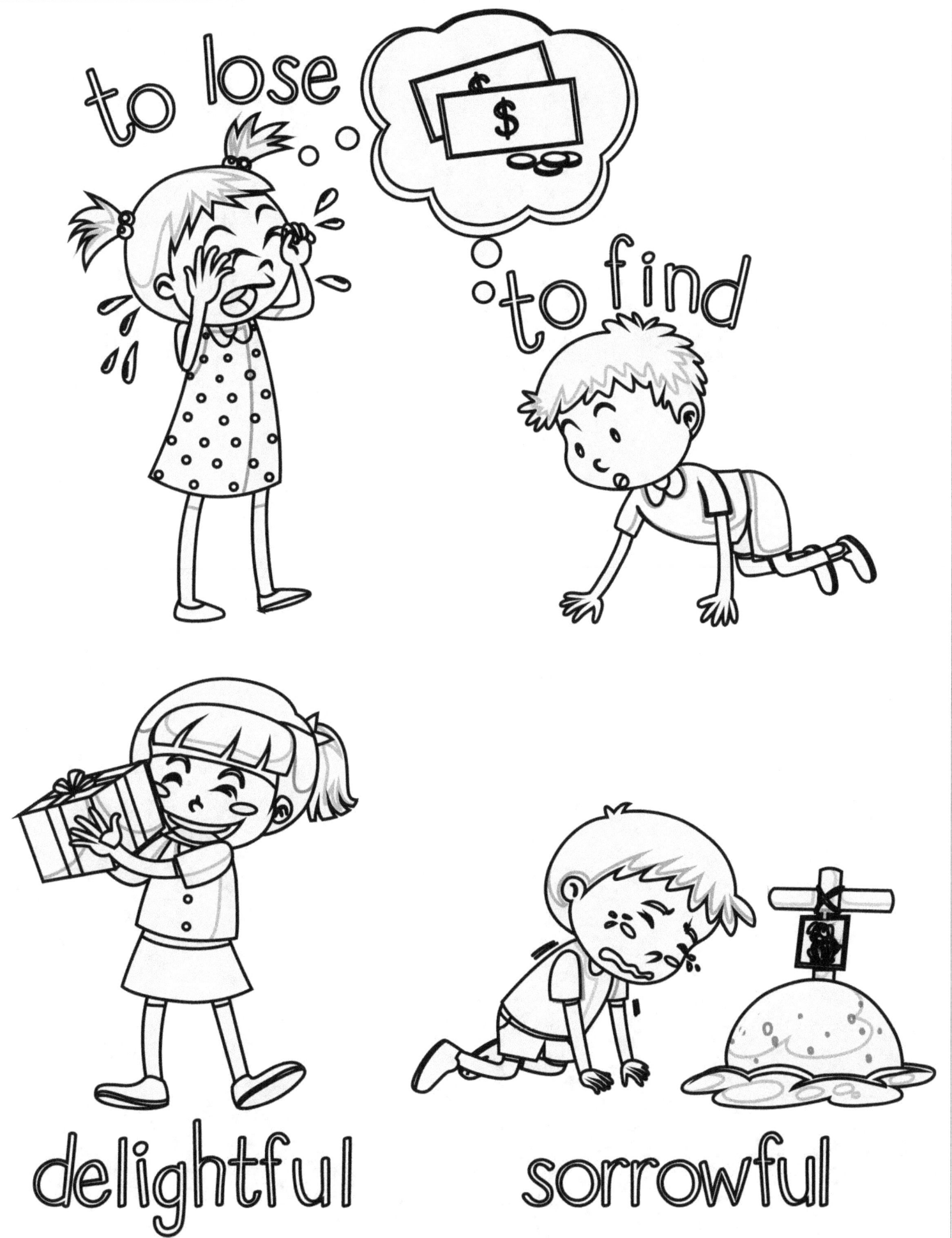

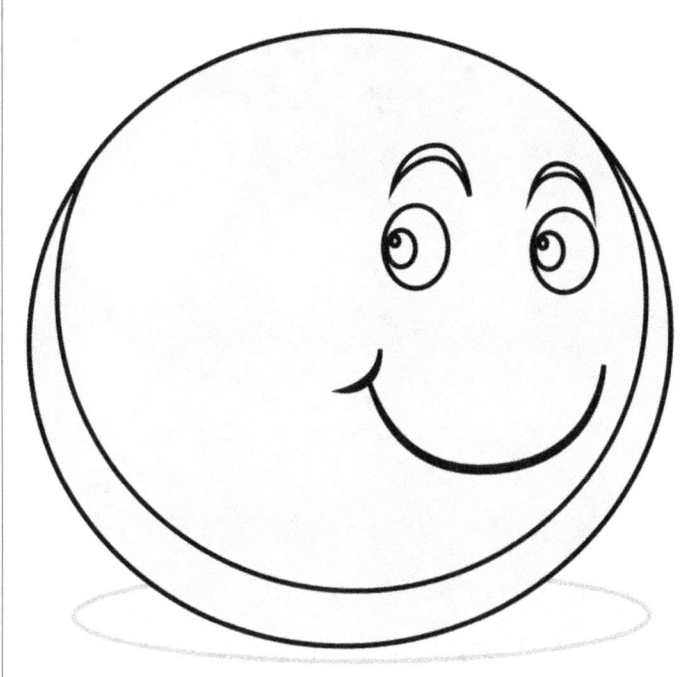 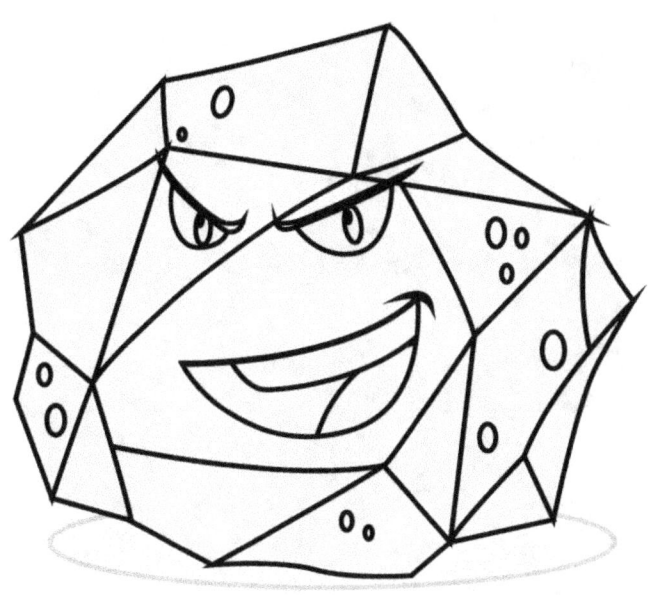

SMOOTH   ROUGH

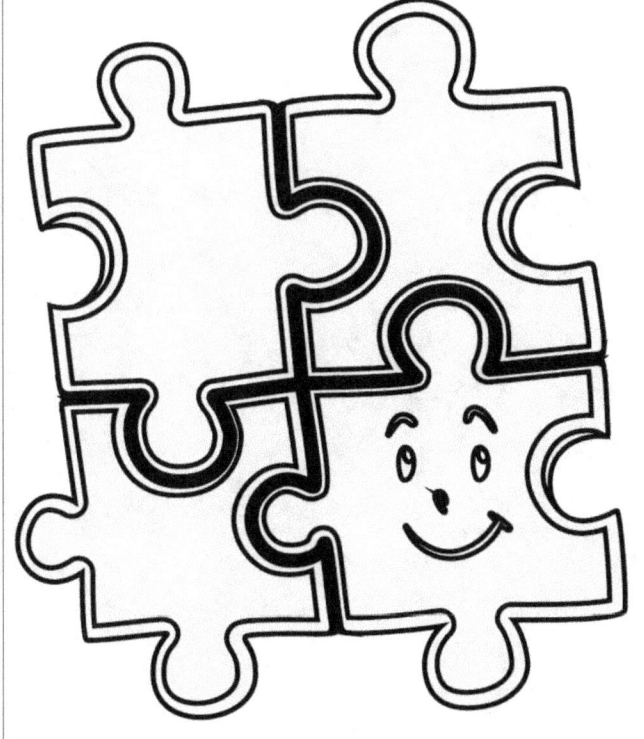 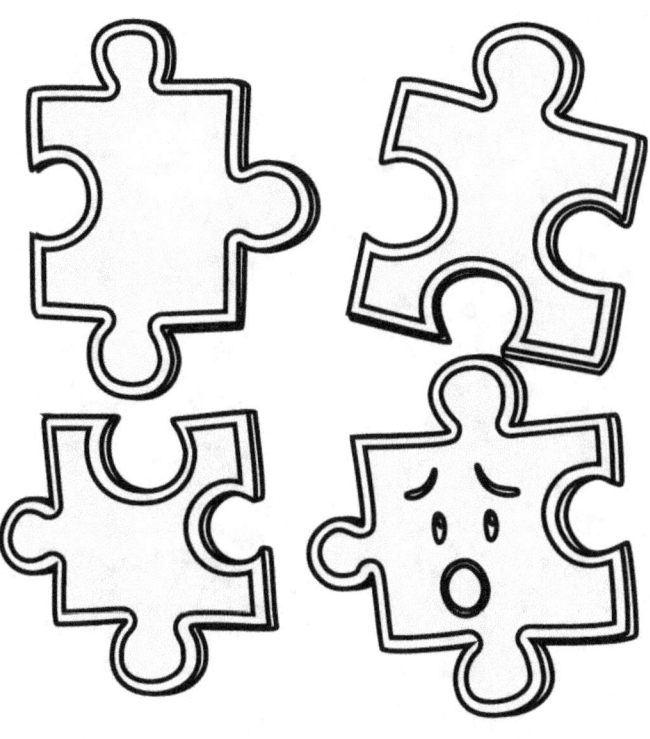

TOGETHER   APART

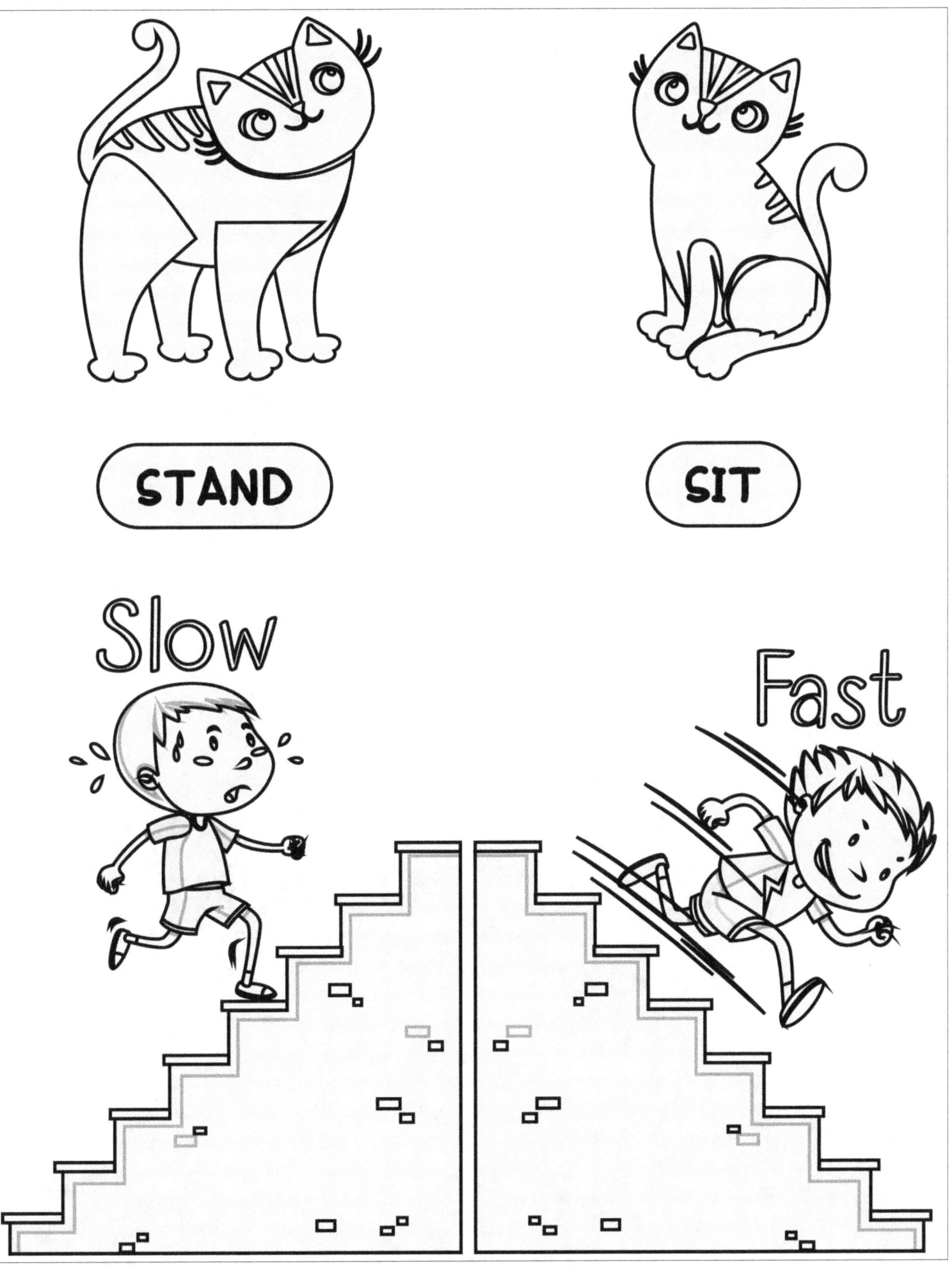

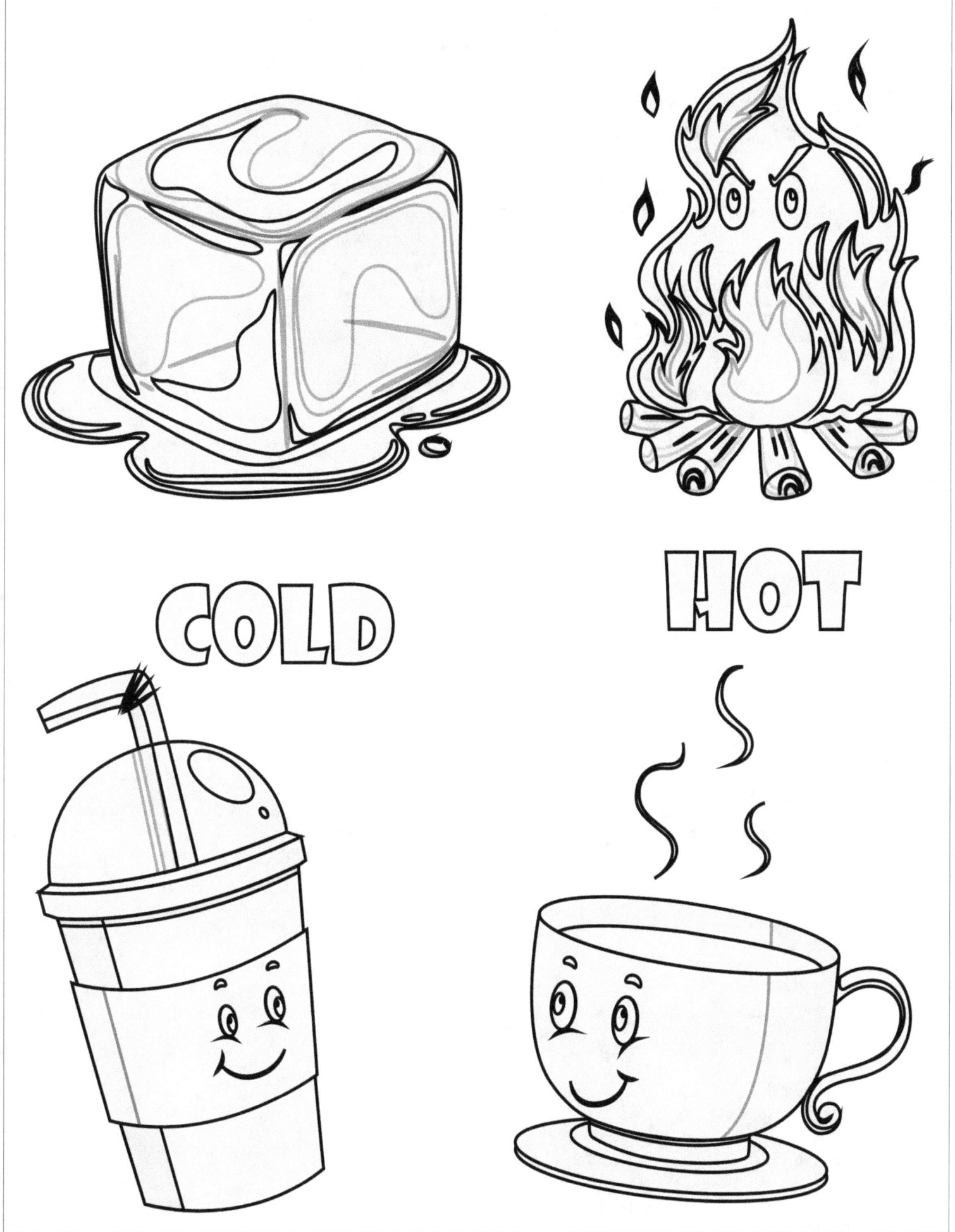

to break   to fix

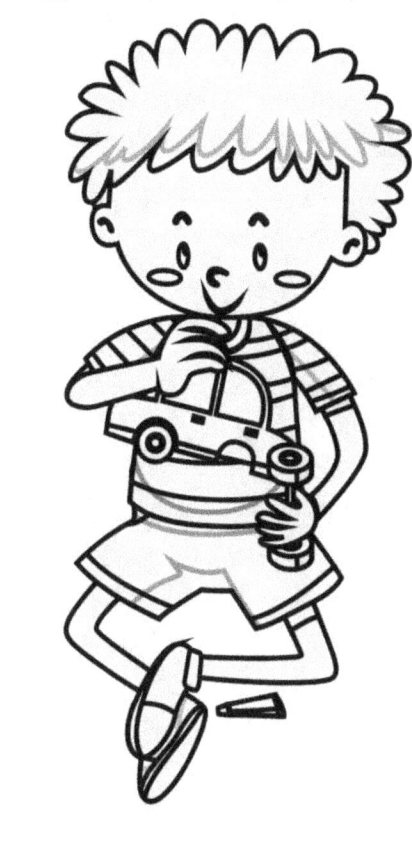

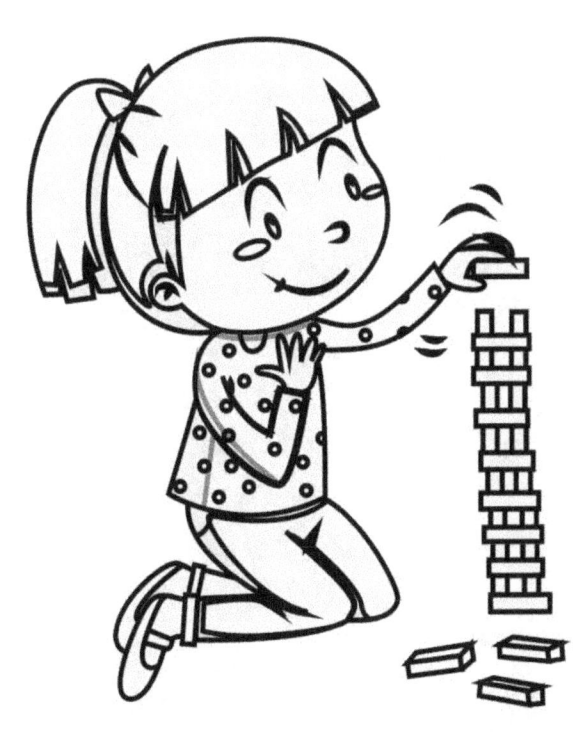
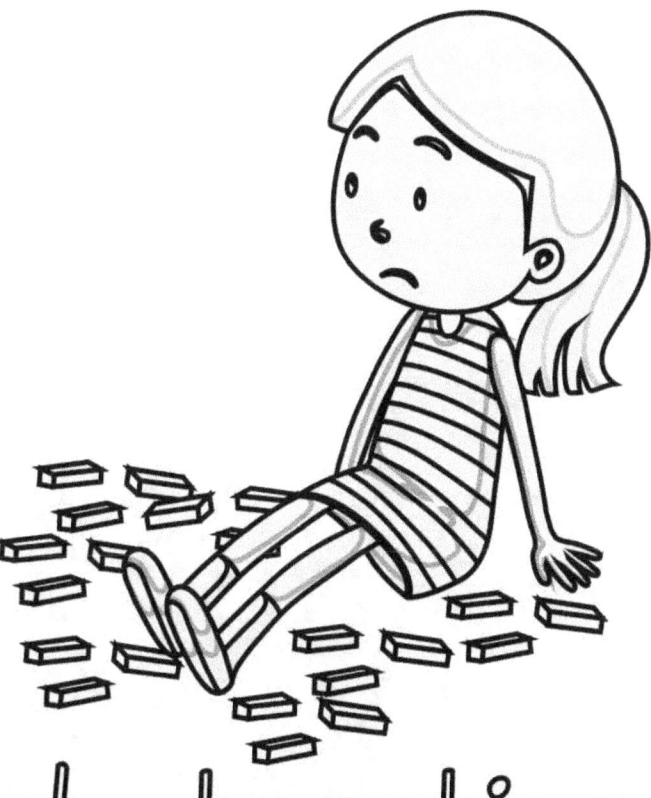

construction   destruction

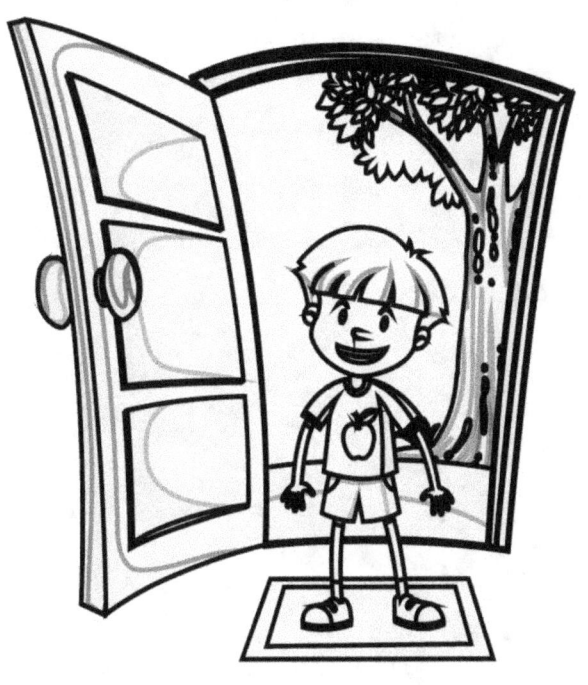
to come

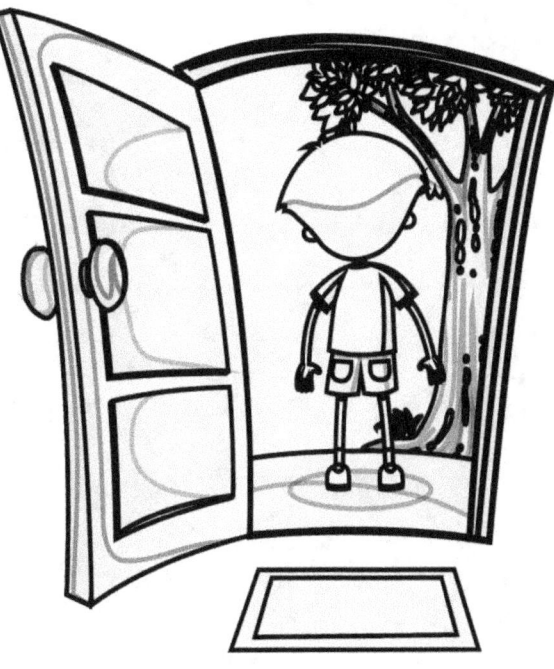
to go

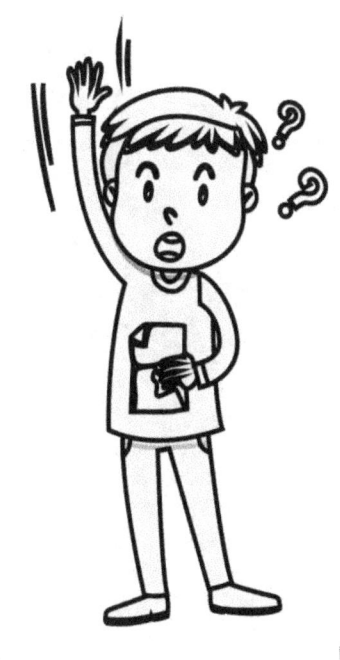
to ask

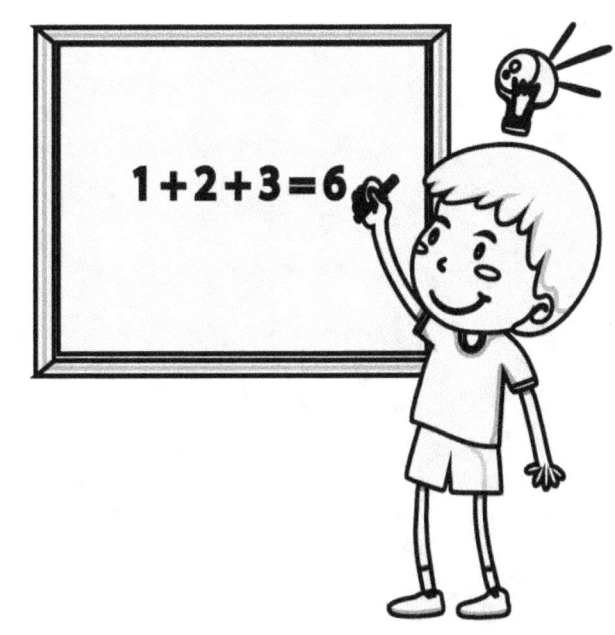
to answer

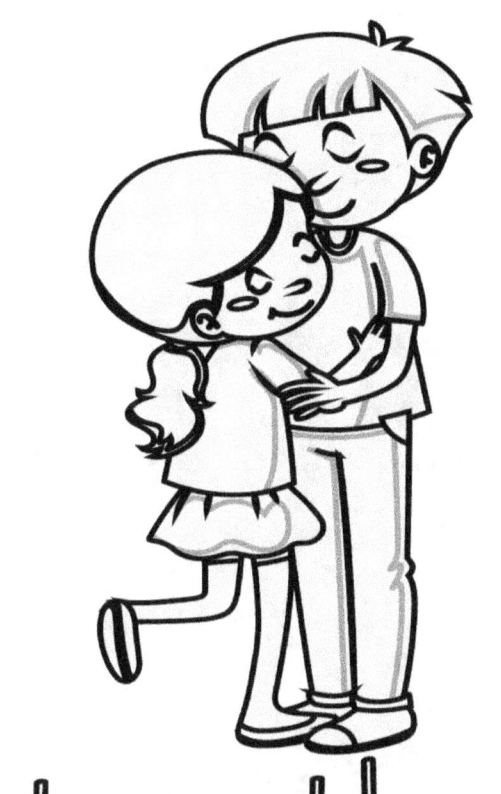 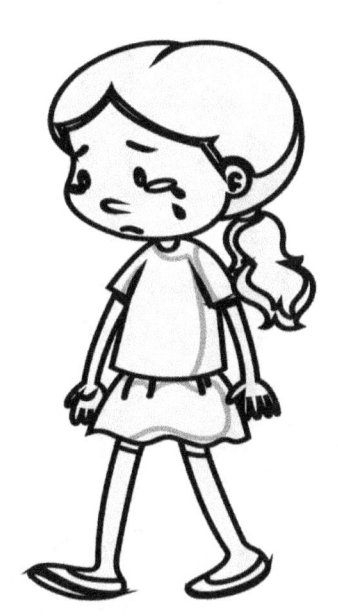 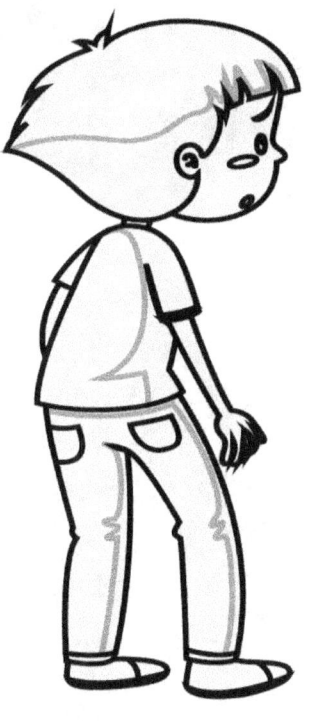

together		apart

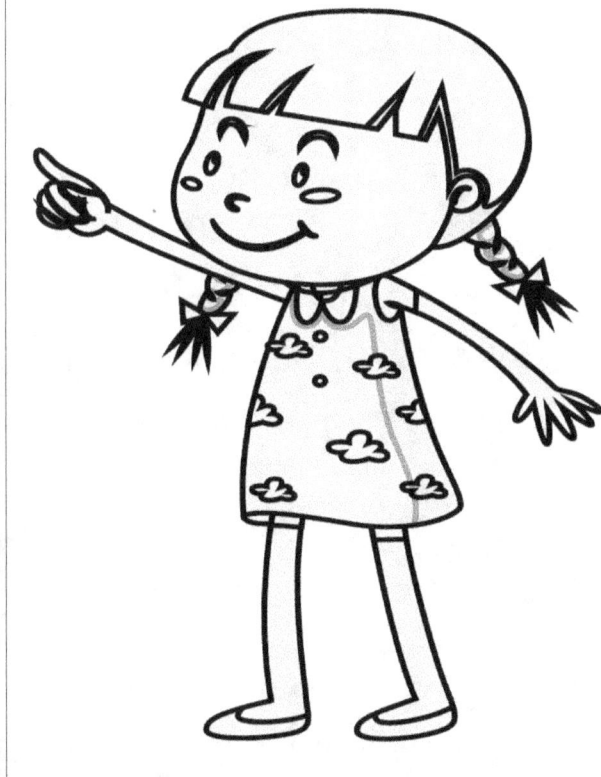 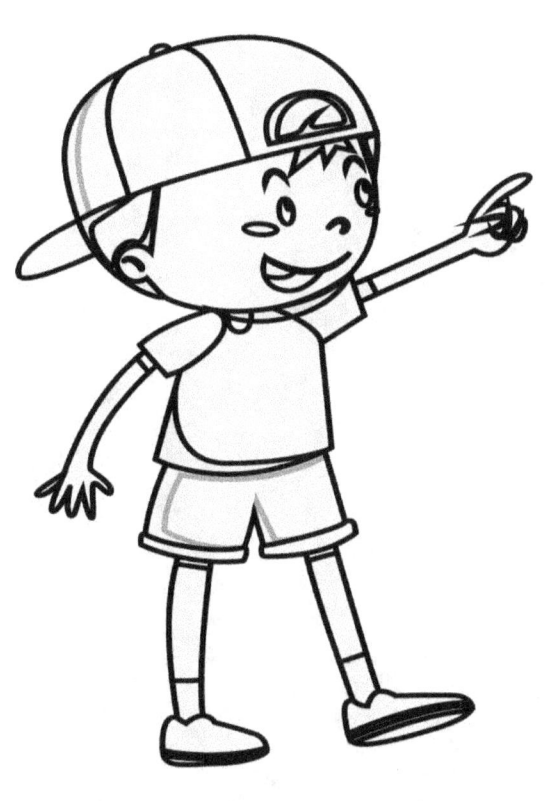

LEFT		RIGHT

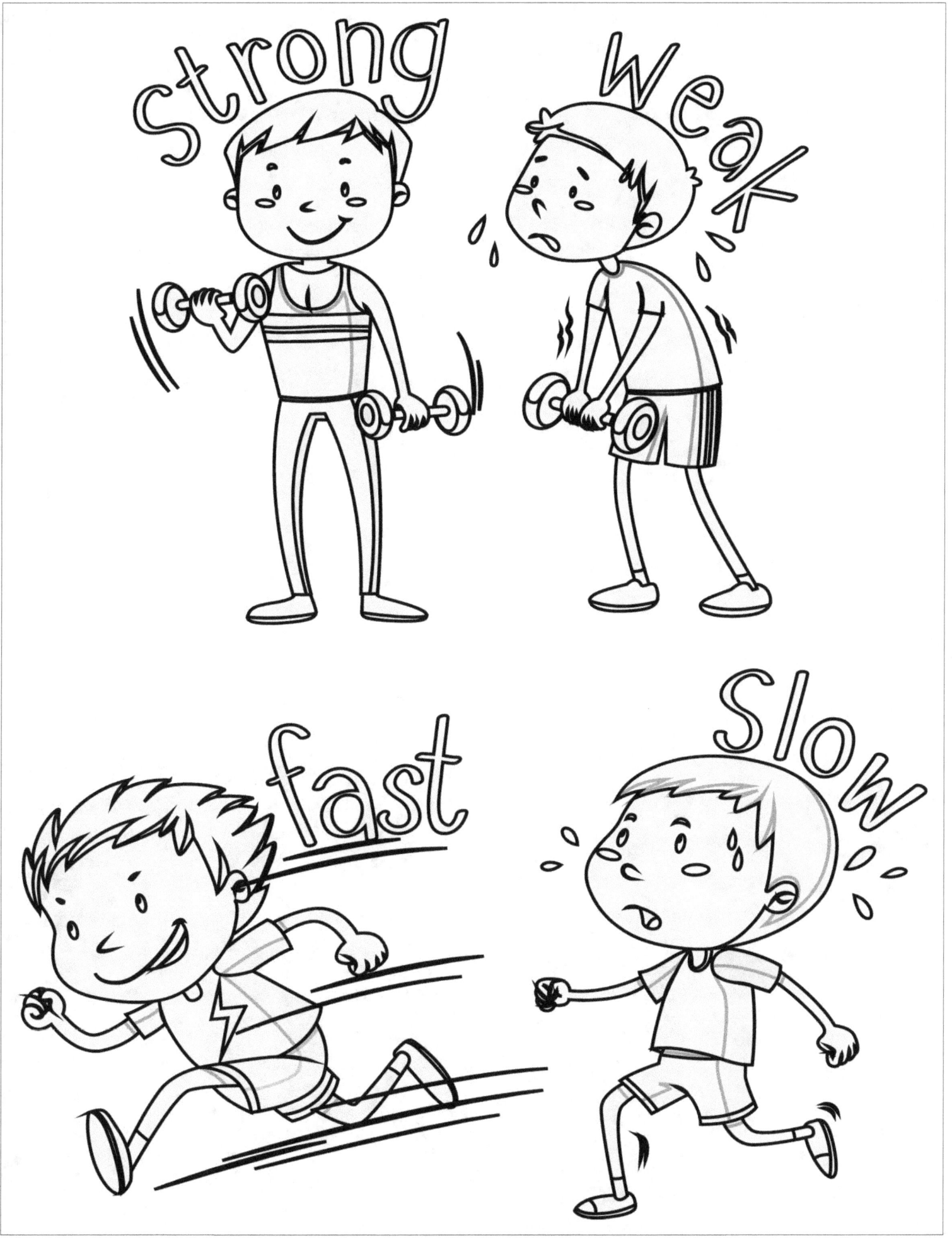

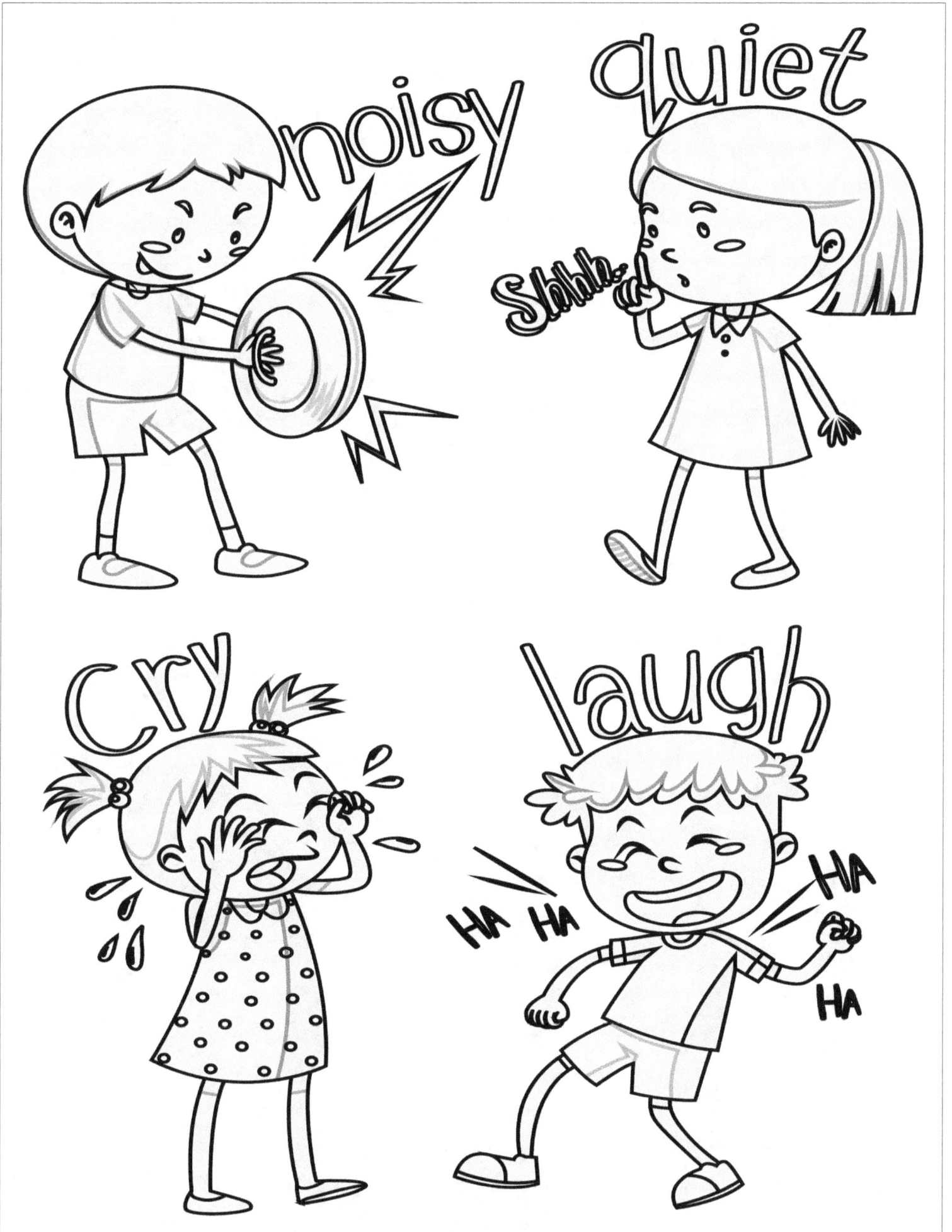

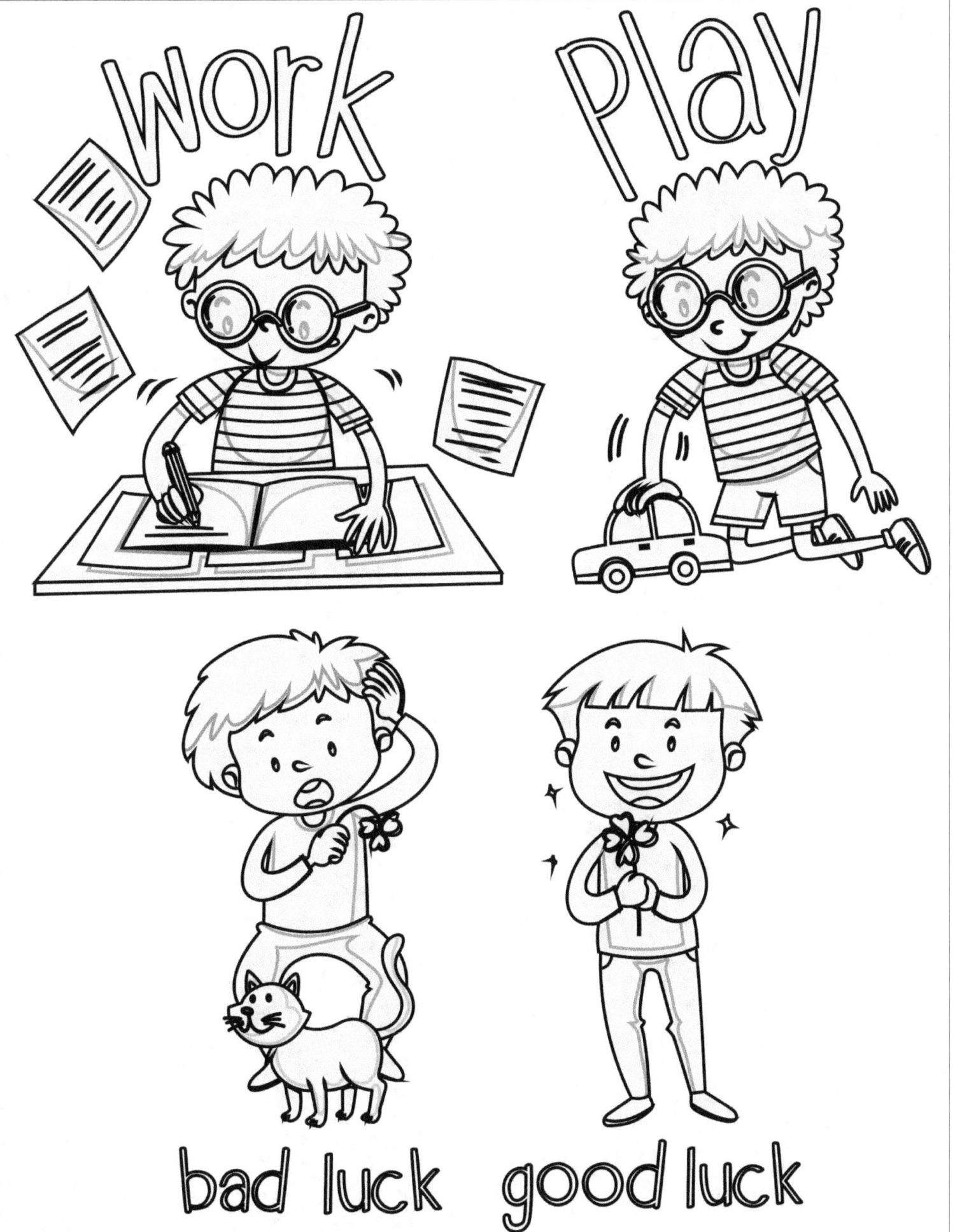

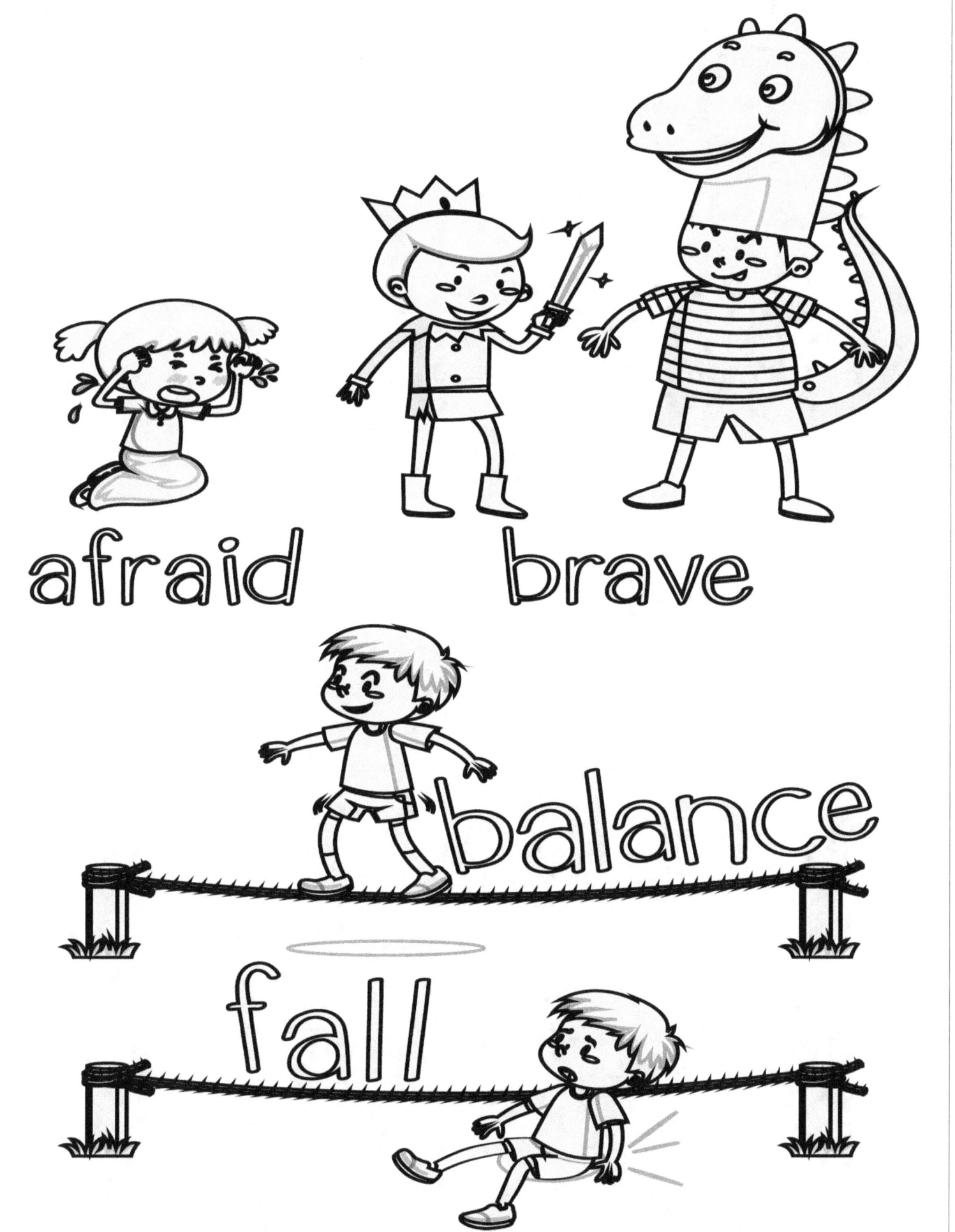

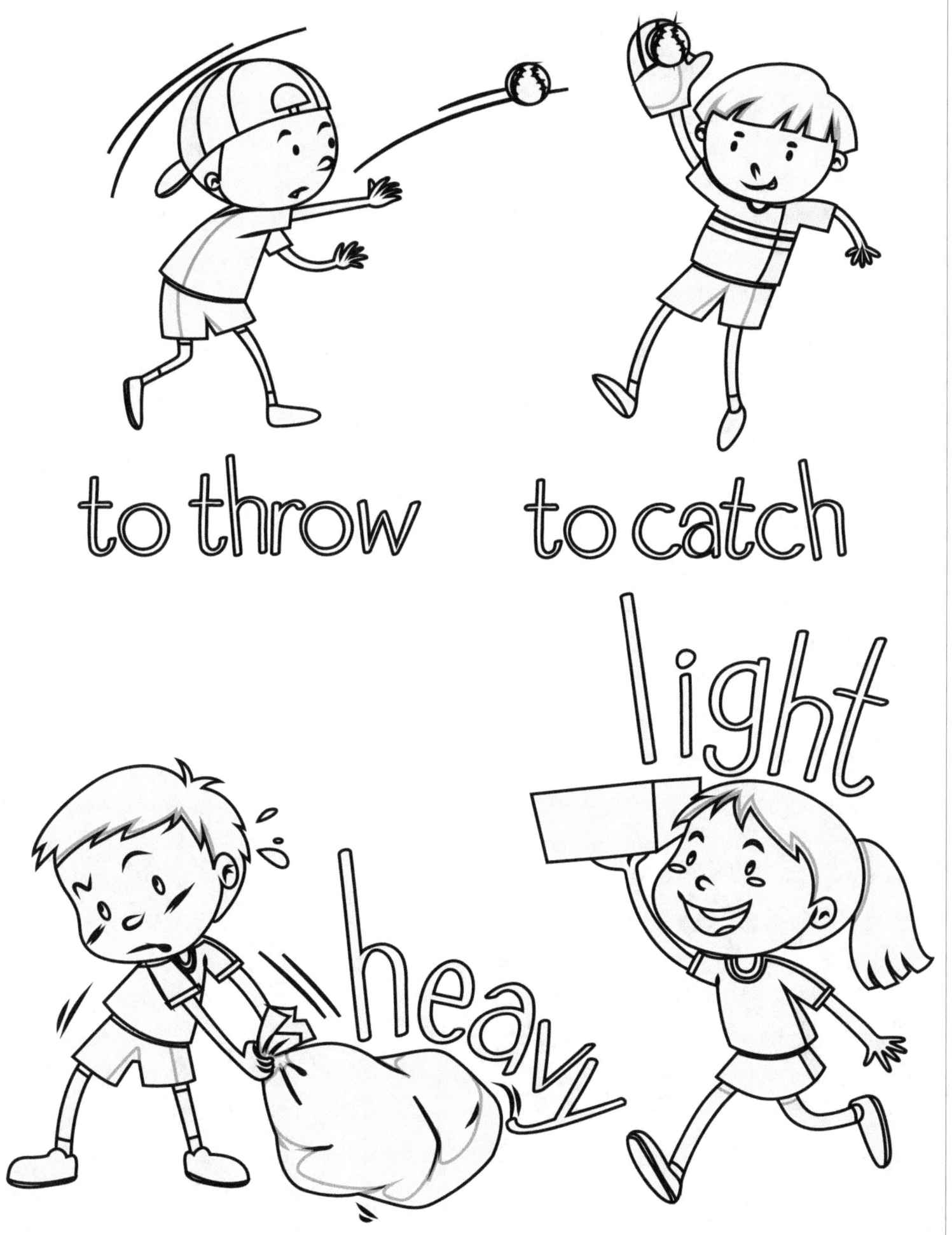

child

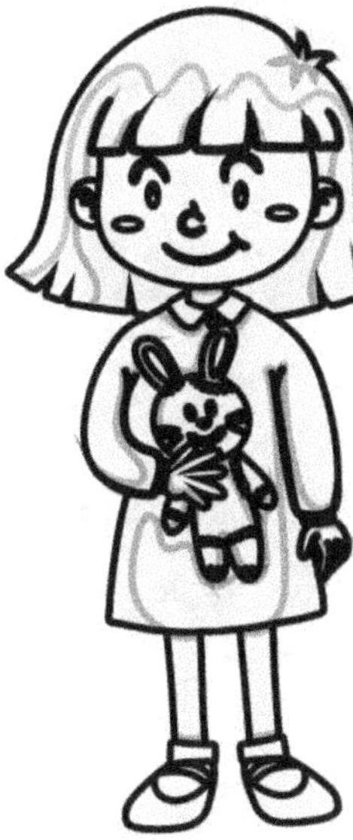

adult

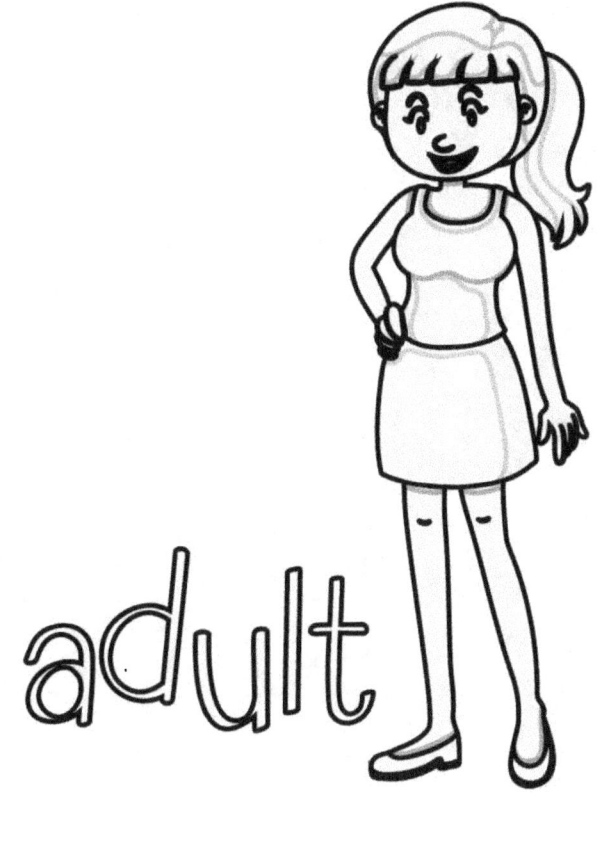

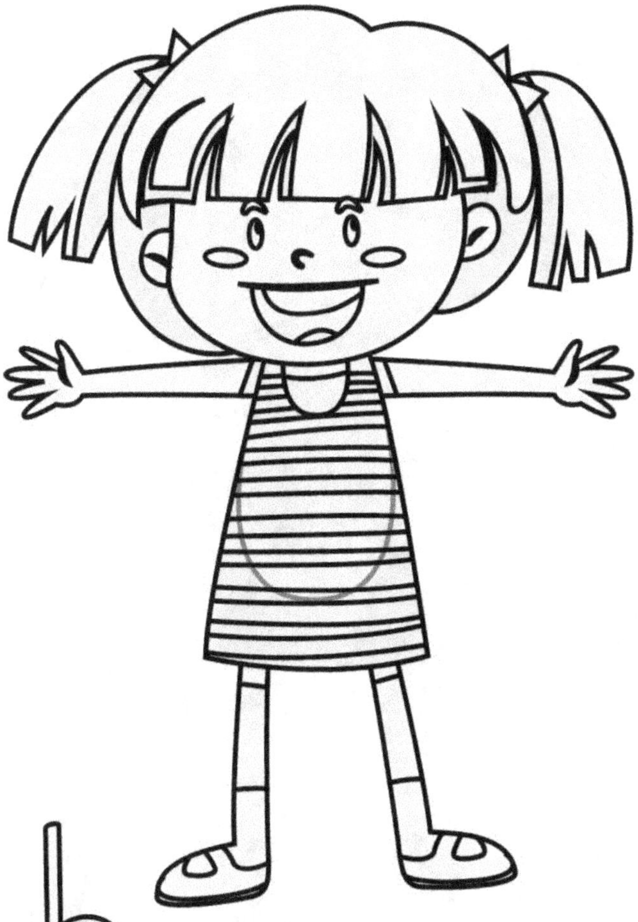

human

animal

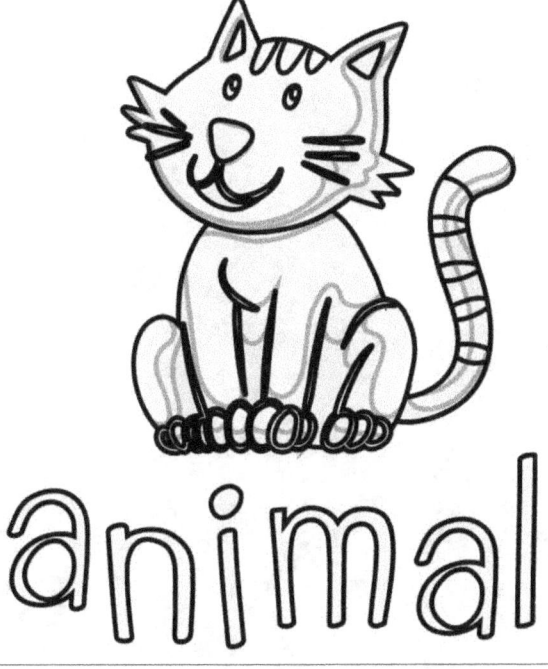

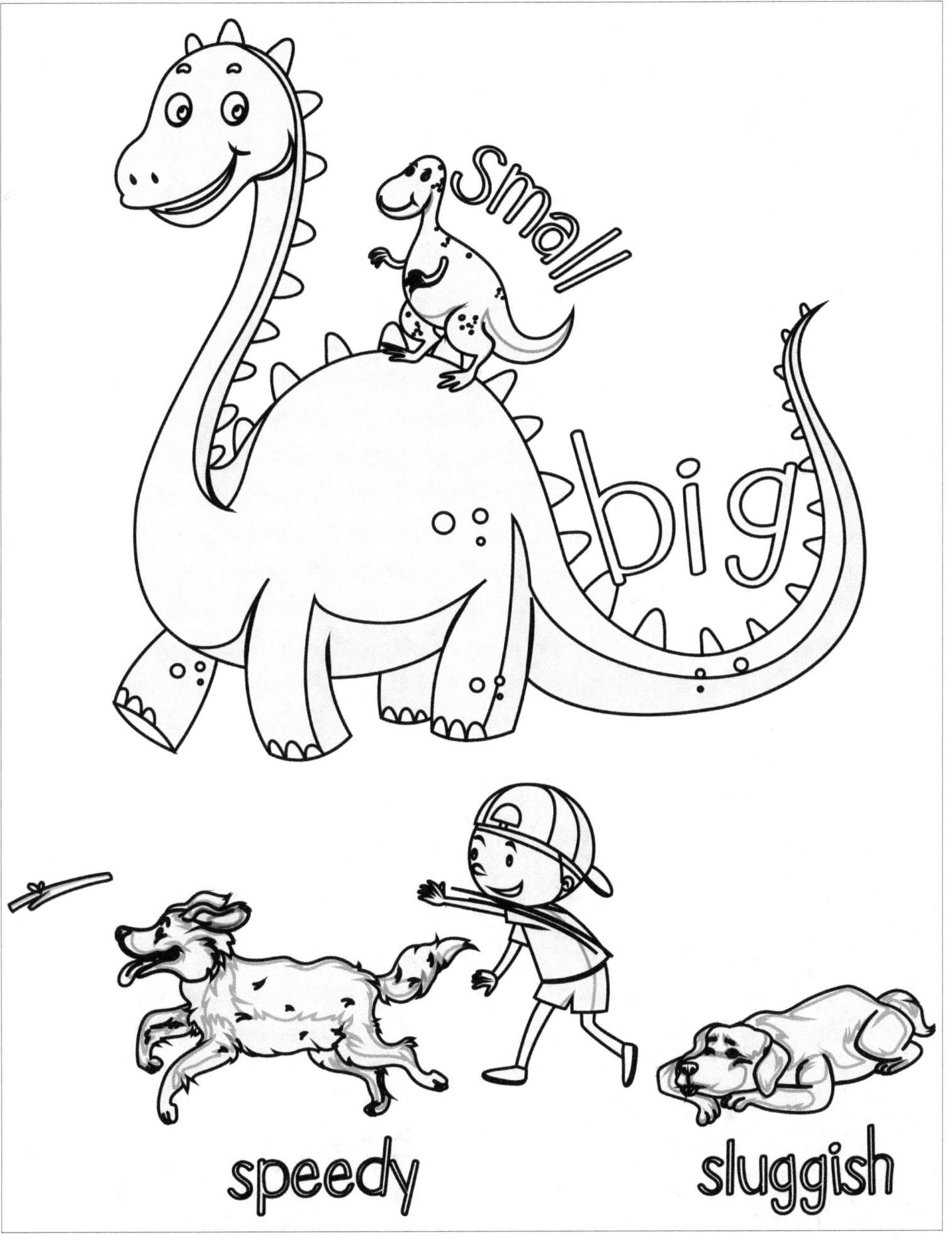

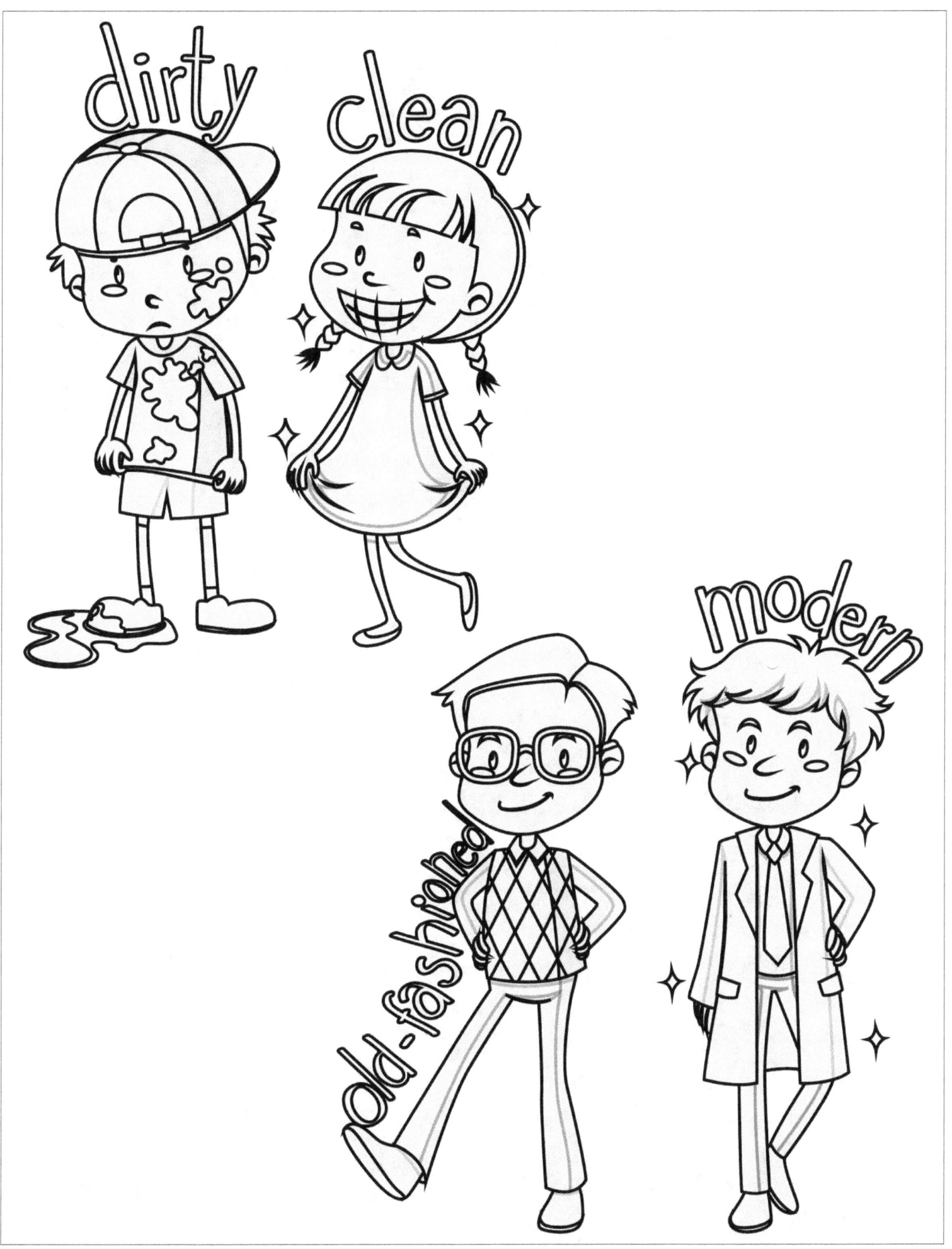

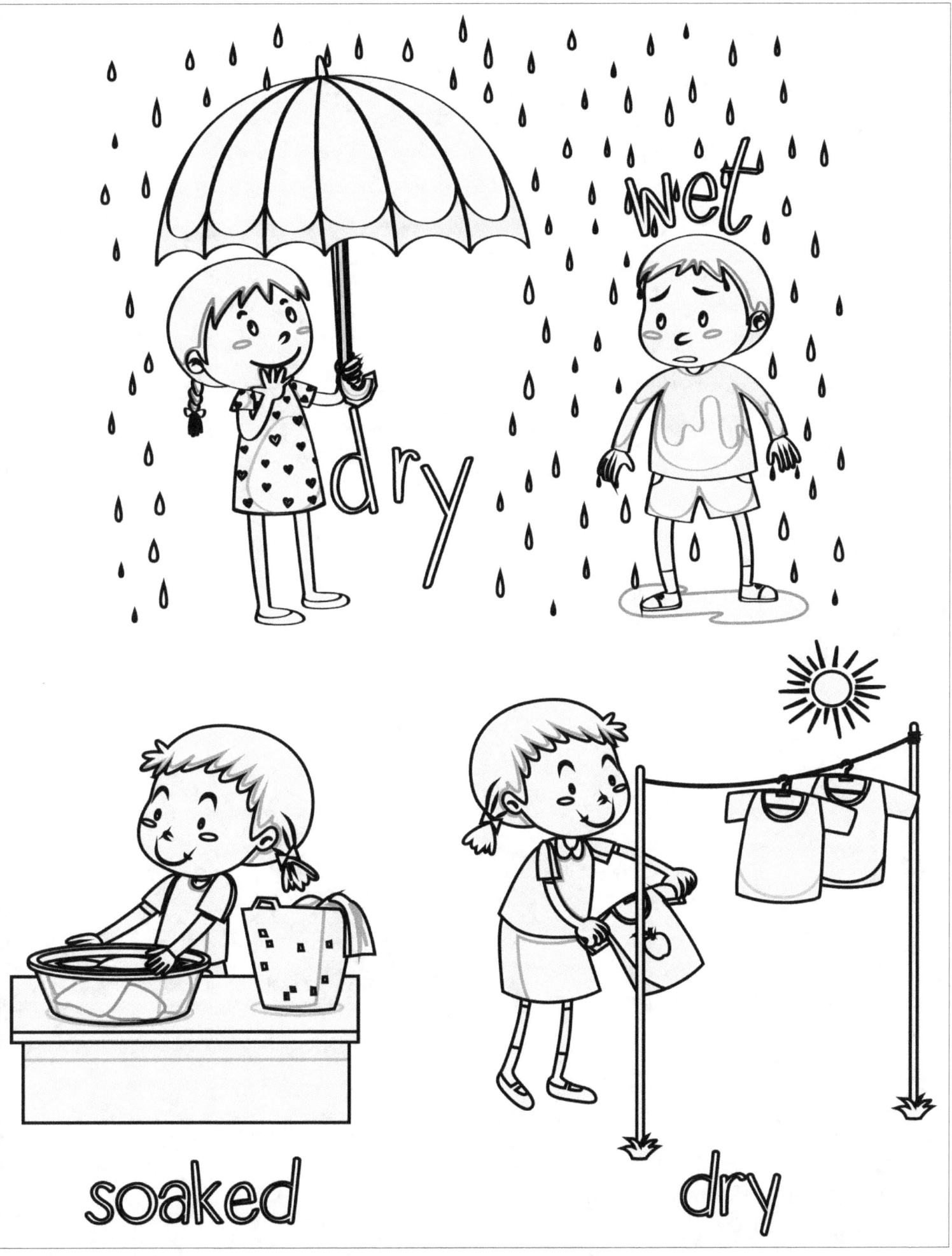

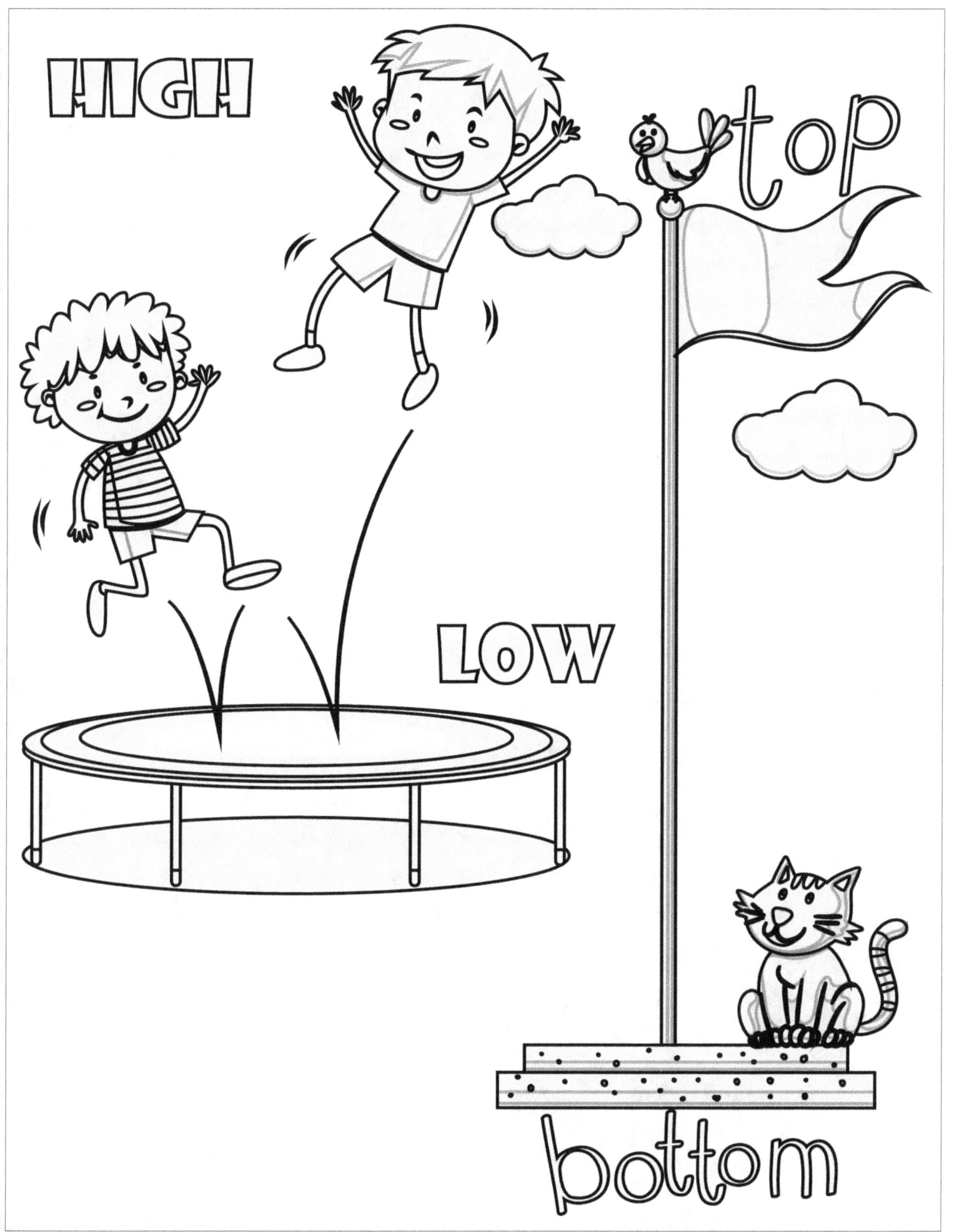

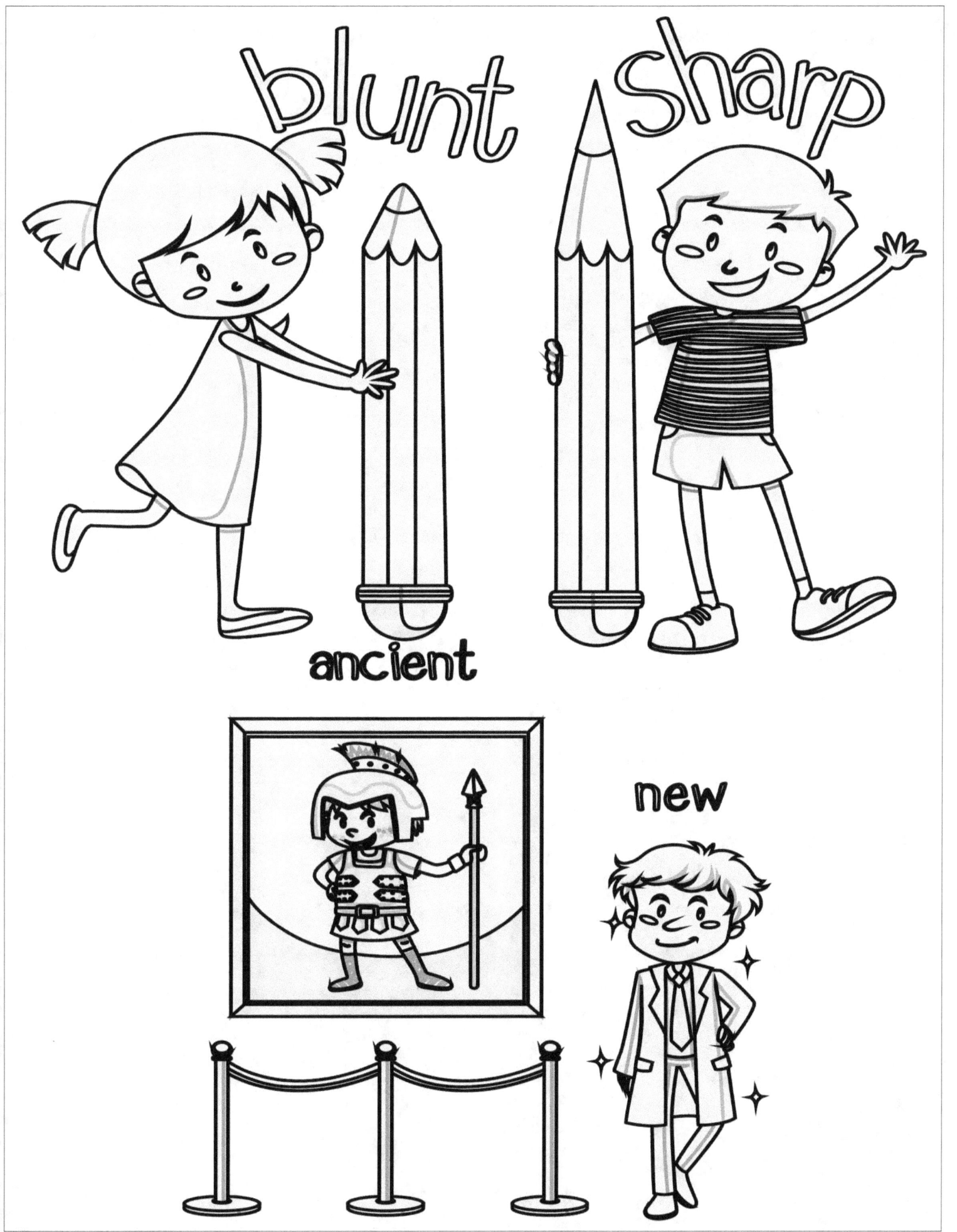

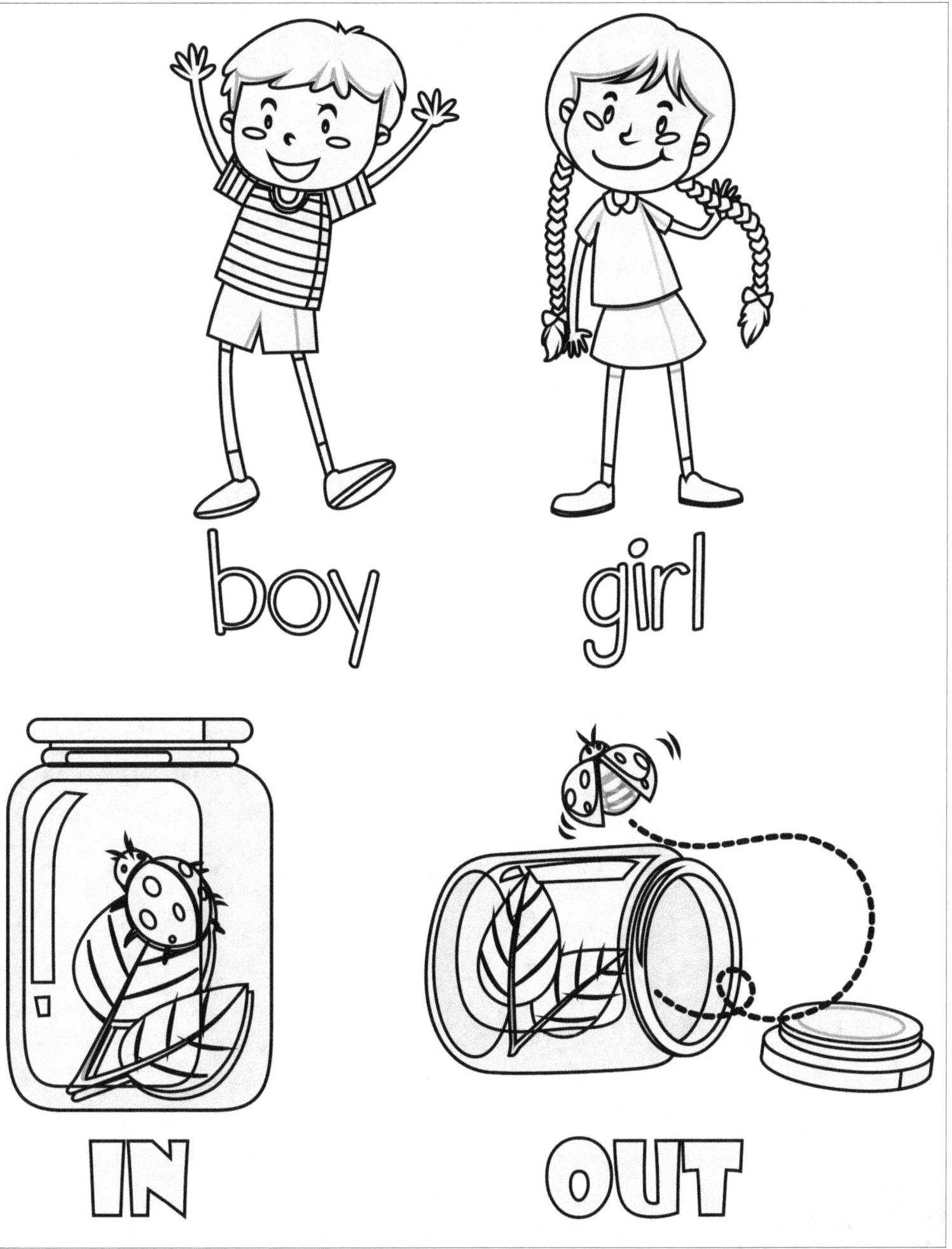

www.ingramcontent.com/pod-product-compliance
Lightning Source LLC
Chambersburg PA
CBHW080502220526
45465CB00006B/2346